ALL YOU NEED TO KNOW....

WORLD WAR II

BY MAX HASTINGS

CONTENTS

To Michael Sissons,
for thirty years a princely agent, counsellor and friend

10 9 8 7 6 5 4 3 2 1

ISBN 978-1-911187-82-0

This is a condensed version of *All Hell Let Loose*, first published in Britain by
HarperPress in 2011

First published as *All you need to know: World War II*
by Connell Publishing in 2018

Picture credits:
p.6 © Popperfoto/Getty Images
pp.10-11 © AP / REX / Shutterstock
pp.22-23 © Pressefoto Kindermann / ullstein bild / Getty Images
pp.76-77 © General Photographic Agency/Getty Images
p.89 © Photo 12 /UIG / Getty Images
p.97 © John Ooney / AP / REX / Shutterstock

Copyright © Max Hastings 2011

Design: Ben Brannan
Typesetting: Paul Woodward
Picture research: Flora Connell
Edited by Jolyon Connell

INTRODUCTION

This is a book chiefly about human experience. Men and women from scores of nations struggled to find words to describe what happened to them in the Second World War, transcending anything they had ever known. Many resorted to a cliché: 'all hell broke loose'. Because the phrase is commonplace in eyewitness descriptions of battles, air raids, massacres and ship sinkings, later generations are tempted to shrug at its banality. Yet in an important sense, the words capture the essence of what the struggle meant to hundreds of millions of people, plucked from peaceful, ordered existences to face ordeals that in many cases lasted for years, and for at least 60 millions were terminated by death. An average of 27,000 people perished each day between September 1939 and August 1945 as a consequence of the global conflict.

Any writer's highest aspiration, more than 65 years after the war's ending, is to offer a personal view rather than a comprehensive account of this greatest and most terrible of all human experiences, which never fails to inspire humility in its modern students, inspired by gratitude that we have been spared from anything comparable. In 1920, when Colonel Charles à Court Repington, military correspondent of *The Daily Telegraph*, published a best-selling account of the recent conflict, it was considered sinister and tasteless that he chose as his title *The First World War*, for it presumed another. To call this book *The Last World War* might tempt providence, but it is at least certain that never again will millions of armed men clash on European battlefields such as those of 1939-45. The conflicts of the future will be quite different, and it may not be rashly optimistic to suggest that they will be less terrible.

CHAPTER ONE

POLAND BETRAYED

While Adolf Hitler was determined to wage war, it was no more inevitable that his 1939 invasion of Poland precipitated global conflict than that the assassination of the Archduke Franz-Ferdinand of Austria did so in 1914. Britain and France lacked both the will and the means to take effective action towards fulfilment of security guarantees they had given earlier to the Poles. Their declarations of war on Germany were gestures which even some staunch anti-Nazis thought foolish, because futile.

At 2000 on the evening of 31 August, 1939, the curtain rose on the first, appropriately sordid act of the conflict. Sturmbannführer Alfred Naujocks of the German SD led a party dressed in Polish uniforms, and including a dozen convicted criminals dismissively codenamed '*Konserven*' – 'tin cans' – in a mock assault on the German radio station at Gleiwitz in Upper Silesia. Shots were fired; Polish patriotic slogans were broadcast across the airwaves; then the 'attackers' withdrew. SS machine-gunners killed the 'tin cans', whose bloodstained corpses were arranged for display to foreign correspondents as evidence of Polish aggression.

At 0200 on 1 September, the Wehrmacht's 1st Mounted Regiment was among scores roused in its bivouacs by a bugle call – some German units as well as many Polish ones rode horses to battle. The squadrons saddled, mounted, and began to move towards their start-line alongside clattering columns of armour, trucks and guns. The order was given: 'Muzzle-caps off! Load! Safety-catches on!' At 0440, the big guns of the old German battleship

Schleswig-Holstein, anchored in Danzig harbour for a 'goodwill visit', opened fire on the Polish fort at Westerplatte.

An hour later, German soldiers tore down crossing-poles on the western frontier, opening the way for leading elements of the invasion force to pour forward into Poland. One of its commanders, General Heinz Guderian, soon found himself passing his family's ancestral estate at Chelmno, where he was born when it formed part of pre-Versailles Germany. Among his soldiers, 23-year-old Lt. Wilhelm Pruller expressed the euphoria which suffused the army: 'It's a wonderful feeling now, to be a German... We've crossed the border. *Deutschland, Deutschland über alles*! The German Wehrmacht is marching!'

The Western Allies, heartened by knowledge that Poland boasted the fourth largest army in Europe, anticipated a struggle lasting some months. The defenders deployed 1.3 million men against 1.5 million Germans, with 37 divisions on each side. But the Wehrmacht was far better equipped, and the Polish Army had held back from full mobilisation in response to Anglo-French pleas to avoid provoking Hitler. Thus, on 1 September, the defenders were surprised.

By the end of the campaign's third week, Polish resistance was broken. The capital, Warsaw, remained unoccupied only because the Germans wished to destroy it before claiming the ruins; hour after hour and day after day, the merciless bombardment continued. A nurse, Jadwiga Sosnkowska, described scenes at her hospital outside Warsaw on 25 September:

> The procession of wounded from the city was an unending march of death. The lights went out, and all of us, doctors and nurses, had to move about with candles in our hands. Tragedy followed tragedy. At one time the victim was a girl of sixteen. She had a glorious mop of golden hair, her face was delicate as a flower, and her lovely sapphire-blue eyes were full of tears... Both her legs, up to the knees, were a mass of bleeding pulp.... Before the surgeon began I bent over this innocent child to kiss her pallid brow, to lay my helpless hand on her golden head. She died quietly in the course of the morning, like a flower plucked by a merciless hand.

Professional soldiers can seldom afford to indulge emotionalism about the horrors of war, but posterity must recoil from the complacency of Germany's generals both about the character of their national leader, and the murderous adventure in which they had become his accomplices. Gen. Erich von

Manstein is widely regarded as the finest German general of the war; after the war, he took pride in pretensions to have done his part as an officer and gentleman. But his writings during the Polish campaign, as well as later, reveal the insensitivity characteristic of his caste. He was delighted by the invasion: 'It's a grand decision of the Führer in view of the attitude of the Western Powers up till now. His offer to solve the Polish question was so obliging that England and France – if they really wanted peace – should have pushed Poland into accepting.'

Manstein signed an order for the German forces encircling Warsaw to fire upon any refugees who attempted to leave: it was deemed easier to force a swift outcome of the campaign, and to avoid a battle in the streets, if the inhabitants were unable to escape the capital's bombardment. Yet he was a man of such personal fastidiousness that he sometimes quit rooms in which Field Marshal Gerd von Rundstedt was speaking, because he recoiled from his chief's obscene language. On 25 September, he basked in a congratulatory visit from Hitler, writing to his wife: 'It was nice to see how the soldiers rejoiced everywhere as the Führer drove past.' In 1939, the officer corps of the Wehrmacht already displayed the moral bankruptcy which would characterise its conduct until 1945.

Poland became the only nation occupied by Hitler in which there was no collaboration between the conquerors and the conquered. The Nazis henceforth classified Poles as slaves, and received in return implacable hatred.

Hitler had committed himself to conquer Poland, but as so often, he had no clear plan for what should follow. Only when it became plain that Stalin welcomed the country's extinction did Germany's ruler decide to annex western Poland. Among his foremost characteristics was a reflexive hatred of all those who opposed his will. This soon manifested itself against the Poles – and especially, of course, against their Jews. One day in Lodz soon after the occupation began, Szmulek Goldberg was returning from work when 'I encountered chaos in the streets. People were running wildly in every direction. Somebody stopped and grabbed my sleeve. "Hide! Hide!" he shrieked. "The Germans are capturing Jews at gunpoint and taking them away on trucks."' He watched trucks drive past, loaded with captives, a first earnest of Hitler's designs upon his race. Within weeks of Poland's conquest, the first few thousand of its Jewish citizens had been murdered.

On 17 September, the Soviet Union had launched its own vicious thrust into eastern Poland, designed to secure Stalin's share of Hitler's booty. Around 1.5 million Poles, mostly civilians evicted from their homes in the forfeited east

HITLER IN POLAND
Hitler salutes parading troops in Warsaw on 5 October 1939

of their country during the months that followed, began an ordeal of captivity and starvation in Soviet hands, which cost the lives of some 350,000. On 5 March 1940, the Soviet Union's security chief Lavrenti Beria sent a four-page memorandum to Stalin, proposing the elimination of Polish senior officers and others defined as leaders of their society. Those held in Soviet camps, urged Beria, should be subjected to 'the use of the highest means of punishment – death by shooting'. During the weeks that followed, at least 25,000 Poles were murdered by NKVD executioners at various Soviet prisons, each receiving a single bullet in the back of the head. The bodies were then buried in mass graves in the forests around Katyn, west of Smolensk, and at other sites, the largest of which was discovered by the gleeful Nazis in 1943. Later allegations that the post-1945 Allied war crimes trials represented 'victors' justice' were powerfully reinforced by the fact that no Russian was ever indicted for Katyn.

Britain and France had declared war on Germany to save Poland. Poland was now gone, and Polish representatives were expelled from the Allied Supreme War Council, where they were deemed redundant. US ambassador in London Joseph Kennedy shrugged to his Polish counterpart: 'Where on earth can the Allies fight the Germans and beat them?' Though Kennedy was a shameless Anglophobe, appeaser and defeatist, his question was valid, and the Allied governments had no good answer to it. Since France and Britain lacked stomach to seize the initiative, the further course of the war waited upon the pleasure of Adolf Hitler.

CHAPTER TWO

BLITZKRIEGS IN THE WEST

Hitler's next conquest was Norway, where the Germans landed on 9 April. The Norwegians, French and British had alike deluded themselves that Hitler would never dare to invade Norway in the face of the Royal Navy. But Norway's nearest coastline lay 400 miles from Britain, beyond range of land-based air cover: the vulnerability of ships to bomber attack was soon brutally exposed.

It is hard to exaggerate the chaos of the Allies' decision-making, or the cynicism of their treatment of the hapless Norwegians. The British government made extravagant promises of aid, while knowing that it lacked means to fulfil them.

The conquest of Norway provided Hitler with naval and air bases which became important when he later invaded Russia. The campaign's most important consequence, however, was that it precipitated the fall of Chamberlain in Britain. Had there been no Norway, it is overwhelmingly likely that he would have retained office as prime minister through the campaign in France which followed. The consequences of such an outcome for Britain, and for the world, could have been catastrophic, because his government might well have chosen a negotiated peace with Hitler.

A month after the invasion of Norway, on the evening of 9 May 1940, French troops on the Western Front heard 'a vast murmuring' in the German lines; word was passed back that the enemy was moving. Commanders chose to believe that this, like earlier such alarms, was false: though the German assault into Holland, Belgium and France began at 0435 on 10 May, it was

0630 before Allied C-in-C General Maurice Gamelin was awakened in his bed, five hours after the first warning from the outposts.

Following the long-anticipated pleas for assistance that now arrived from governments in Brussels and the Hague, neutrals in the path of the German storm, Gamelin ordered an advance to the river Dyle in Belgium, fufilling his longstanding contingency plan. The British Expeditionary Force's nine divisions and the best of France's forces began rolling north-eastwards. The Luftwaffe made no serious attempt to interfere, for this was exactly where Hitler wanted the Allies to go; their departure removed a critical threat to the flank of the main German armies, which were thrusting forward further south.

The defences of Holland and Belgium were smashed open: in the first hours of 10 May, glider-landed Luftwaffe paratroops secured the vital Eben Emael fort, covering the Albert Canal in Belgium. Even as Churchill took up office as Britain's prime minister, German spearheads were rolling up the Dutch Army. Meanwhile, south-westwards, some 134,000 men and 1,600 vehicles, of which 1,222 were tanks, began threading their way through the Ardennes forest to deliver the decisive blow of the campaign against the weak centre of the French line. Germans joked afterwards that they created 'the greatest traffic jam in history' in the woods of Luxemburg and southern Belgium, forcing thousands of tanks, trucks and guns along narrow roads the Allies had deemed wholly unsuitable for moving an army.

It is untrue that France's defence rested chiefly on the frontier fortifications of the Maginot Line: the chief purpose of its bunkers and guns was to liberate men for active operations further north. Scarred by memories of the 1914-18 devastation and slaughter in their own country, the French were bent upon waging war somewhere other than on their own soil: Gamelin planned a decisive battle in Belgium, heedless of the fact that the Germans had other ideas. The French response was painfully sluggish, absurdly complacent. It was suggested to Gen. Huntzinger that the German assault was unfolding like that on Poland. The Frenchman shrugged theatrically: 'Poland is Poland... Here we are in France.'

The disparity between the battlefield performance of the German and western Allied armies would prove one of the great enigmas not merely of the 1940 campaign, but of the entire conflict. The Wehrmacht, recreated in the 1930s from a mere cadre, had prepared and conditioned itself solely for continental war. Its officers displayed greater energy, professionalism and imagination than most of their British counterparts; its men proved highly motivated. An institutional discipline pervaded the German Army's battlefield conduct at every level, and persisted throughout the war. Its commitment

DUNKIRK
British soldiers wade out to a waiting destroyer

to counter-attack, even in adverse circumstances, amounted to genius. The concept of conducting war *a l'outrance*, pursuing to the last gasp the destruction of the enemy, seemed to come naturally to Germans, as it did not to their British or French enemies. On the battlefield Allied soldiers, reflecting the societies from which they were drawn, prided themselves on behaving like reasonable men. The Wehrmacht showed what unreasonable men could do.

The Royal Navy's achievement in evacuating the British Expeditionary Force from Dunkirk after the fall of France became the stuff of legend. Vice-Admiral Bertram Ramsay, operating from an underground headquarters at Dover, directed the movements of almost 900 ships and small craft with extraordinary calm and skill. The removal of troops from the beaches in civilian launches and pleasure boats forged the romantic image of Dunkirk, but by far the larger proportion – some two-thirds – were taken off by destroyers and other large vessels, loading at the harbour. The navy was fortunate that, throughout the week, the Channel remained almost preternaturally calm.

Soldier Arthur Gwynn-Browne poured out in lyrical terms his gratitude for finding himself returning home from the alien hell of Dunkirk: 'It was so wonderful. I was on a ship and any ship yes any ship is England... I kept quite still and the sea breezes I swallowed them, no smoke and burning... I was alive it was so wonderful.'

The navy suffered severely at Dunkirk, losing six destroyers and a further 25 damaged. But the towering reality was that the BEF got away. Some 338,000 men were brought back to England, 229,000 of them British, the remainder French and Belgian.

Dunkirk was indeed a deliverance, from which the prime minister extracted a perverse propaganda triumph. The British Army salvaged a professional cadre around which new formations might be built, but all its arms and equipment had been lost. The BEF left behind in France 64,000 vehicles, 76,000 tons of ammunition, 2,500 guns and more than 400,000 tons of stores. Britain's land forces were effectively disarmed: many soldiers would wait years before receiving weapons and equipment which rendered them once more fit for a battlefield.

Winston Churchill was almost alone among Anglo-French directors of the war in being willing to wage war *a l'outrance*, to demand a struggle to the last man. French politicians and generals, by contrast, adopted a rationalist view: they identified limits to the damage acceptable to the population and fabric of their country to avoid bowing to a foreign invader, as often before in history France had been compelled to bow. Very few Frenchmen in 1940 and afterwards followed the example set by tens of thousands of Poles – fighting on in exile, even after their country had been defeated.

CHAPTER THREE

BRITAIN ALONE

R AF fighter pilot Paul Richey, wounded in France, was flown home by mail plane in the first days of June 1940:

I looked down on the calm and peaceful English countryside, the smoke rising not from bombed villages, but lazily from cottage chimneys, and saw a game of cricket in progress on a village pitch. With my mind still filled with the blast and flame that had shattered France, I was seized with utter disgust at the smug contentedness England enjoyed behind her sea barrier. I thought a few bombs might wake up those cricketers, and that they wouldn't be long in coming either.

Richey echoed the resentment many men and women feel, on coming fresh from the horrors of war to encounter those spared from them. He was right that the people of southern England would not long enjoy their cricket undisturbed. But, when summoned from their pitches, almost without comprehension until their national leader enthroned their experience in majestic prose, they inflicted upon Hitler's Germany one of the great defeats of history.

It is striking to contrast the prime minister's appeal in his famous speech to the House of Commons on 18 June 1940 to 'brace ourselves to our duties' with the strident demands of Germany's warlord, in similar circumstances in 1944-45, for 'fanatical resistance'. Grace, dignity, wit, humanity and resolution characterised the leadership of Britain's prime minister; only the last of these could be attributed to Hitler. In the summer of 1940, Churchill faced an enormous challenge, to convince his own people and the world that continued resistance was credible.

The latter months of the year were decisive in determining the course of the war: the Nazis, stunned by the scale of their triumphs, allowed themselves to suffer a loss of momentum. By launching an air assault on Britain, Hitler adopted the worst possible strategic compromise. As master of the continent, he believed a modest further display of force would suffice to precipitate Britain's surrender. Yet if, instead, he had left Churchill's people to stew in their island, the prime minister would have faced great difficulties in sustaining national morale and a charade of strategic purpose.

As it was, however, the Luftwaffe's clumsy offensive posed the one challenge which Britain was well-placed to repel. The British Army and people were not obliged to confront the Wehrmacht on their beaches and in their fields – a clash which would probably have ended ignominiously. The prime minister merely required their acquiescence, while the country was defended by a few hundred RAF pilots and – more importantly though less conspicuously – by the formidable might of the Royal Navy's ships at sea. The prime minister's exalting leadership secured public support for his defiance, even when cities began to burn and civilians to die.

The Luftwaffe air assault on Britain which began in July 1940 offered Churchill's people their best opportunity to engage the Germans on favourable terms. The only class of weapons system in which the British had near-parity with their enemies in quality and quantity was the single-seat interceptor fighter. The RAF's Hurricanes and Spitfires were handicapped by clumsy tactical doctrine and .303 machine-gun armament with inadequate destructive power, but squadrons were controlled by the most sophisticated radar, ground observer and voice radio network in the world, created by an inspired group of civil servants, scientists and airmen. If the equipment and performance of Britain's army remained unsatisfactory throughout the war, Churchill's nation far surpassed Germany in the application of science and technology: mobilisation of the best civilian brains, and their integration into the war effort at the highest levels, was an outstanding British success story. The RAF had developed a remarkable system of defence, while their opponents had no credible system of attack.

The Luftwaffe sought to gain dominance of the air space over south-east England by destroying Fighter Command, and embarked on an incoherent campaign to achieve this by sending bombers to attack airfields and installations, escorted by fighters which were expected to shoot down RAF planes as

WINSTON CHURCHILL
Churchill in Downing Street giving his famous 'V' sign.

easily as they had done in France. Intelligence, a chronic weakness of the Third Reich, was woeful: the Germans had no understanding of Fighter Command's detection and control network. Throughout the war, institutionalised hubris dogged the Nazi leadership, which was repeatedly wrong-footed by Allied technological initiatives.

The Germans conducted the Battle of Britain with stunning incompetence, founded upon arrogance and ignorance. If the RAF made its share of mistakes, Air Chief Marshal Sir Hugh Dowding and his most important subordinate, Air Vice-Marshal Keith Park, displayed a steadiness of judgement amounting to brilliance, entirely absent across the Channel. The Germans began their campaign with two assets: a modest superiority of aircraft numbers and a corps of experienced combat veterans. They failed to concentrate these, however, against the vital targets – radar receivers, fighter stations and supporting installations.

At the end of August, they made their worst strategic mistake of the campaign: they shifted their objectives from airfields first to London, then to other major cities. Hitler's air commanders believed this would force Dowding to commit his last reserves; but Britain's leaders, from Churchill downwards, were vastly relieved.

Hitler might have attempted an invasion of Britain if the Luftwaffe had secured control of the air space over the Channel and southern England. As it was, Churchill exploited the threat more effectively than did the prospective invaders, mobilising every citizen to the common purpose of resisting the enemy if they landed. Signposts and place names were removed from crossroads and stations, beaches wired, over-age and under-age men recruited to local 'Home Guard' units and provided with simple weapons.

On 17 September Hitler gave the order indefinitely to postpone Operation *Sealion*; he committed his air force instead to a protracted assault on Britain's cities. The 'blitz' was far harder for Fighter Command to repel than daylight attacks, because the RAF had few night fighters and only primitive Air Interception radar. It inflicted heavy damage on British city centres and ate deep into the spirits of millions of people who endured many nights huddled in shelters with their families and fears.

But Hitler's air assault on Britain ranks second only to the invasion of Russia among his great blunders of the war. After June 1940 many of Churchill's people, especially in high places, recognised their country's inability to challenge Nazi mastery of the continent; if they had merely been left to contemplate British impotence, political agitation for a negotiation with Germany might well have been renewed, and gained support from the old appeasers still holding high government office.

Save for a small force dispatched to North Africa, between late June 1940 and April 1941 scarcely a single German soldier fired a shot in anger. There was a protracted lull in ground operations, a loss of impetus unapparent at the time but critical to the course of the war. The German navy was too weak either to support an invasion of Britain or to sever its Atlantic lifeline; the Luftwaffe's campaign against Britain had failed. It seems almost frivolous to suggest that Hitler determined to invade Russia because he could not think what else to do, but there is something in this, as Ian Kershaw has observed. Many more Nazi battlefield triumphs lay ahead, but some German generals privy to their Führer's intentions already understood the Third Reich's fundamental difficulty: anything less than hemispheric domination threatened disaster; yet its military and economic capability to achieve this remained doubtful. If Britain at the end of 1940 was still beleaguered, Germany's might rested on foundations much weaker than the world supposed.

CHAPTER FOUR

BARBAROSSA

At 0315 Berlin time on 22 June 1941, Russian border guards on the Bug river bridge at Kolden were summoned by their German counterparts 'to discuss important matters' and machine-gunned as they approached. Wehrmacht sappers tore away charges laid on the railway bridge at Brest-Litovsk, then waved forward the assault units at 0330. Some 3.6 million Axis troops began to advance into the Soviet Union on a 900-mile front from the Baltic to the Black Sea, smashing into the defences with devastating effect.

Hitler's invasion of the Soviet Union was the defining event of the war, just as the Holocaust was the defining act of Nazism. The historian Michael Howard has written:

> Many, perhaps most Germans, and certainly most German intellectuals, saw the First World War as a battle for cultural survival against the converging forces of Russian barbarism and, far more subversive, the decadent civilisation of the West, embodied no longer by French aristocrats but by the materialist societies of the Anglo-Saxon world. This belief was taken over in its entirety by the Nazis and provided the bedrock of their own philosophy.

Millions of young Germans had been conditioned since childhood to believe that their nation faced an existential threat from the Soviet Union. Eighteen-year-old Henry Metelmann, a Hamburg locksmith turned tank driver, wrote

BARBAROSSA
German troops on the move in June 1941

later: 'I accepted as natural that it was a German duty for the good of humanity to impose our way of life on lower races and nations who, probably because of their limited intelligence, would not quite understand what we were on about.'

Stalin probably intended to fight his menacing neighbour at some moment of his choosing. As it was, in 1941 his armies were unfit to face the almost undivided attentions of the Wehrmacht.

In Hitler's terms, this made Operation *Barbarossa* a rational act, enabling Germany to engage the Soviet Union while its own relative advantage was greatest. Hubris lay in its underestimate of the military and industrial capability Stalin had already achieved; reckless insouciance about Russia's almost limitless expanses; and grossly inadequate logistical support for a protracted campaign. It did not occur to Hitler, after his victories in the West, that it might be more difficult to overcome a brutalised society, inured to suffering, than democracies such as France and Britain, in which moderation and respect for human life were deemed virtues.

The senior officers of the Wehrmacht flattered themselves that they represented a cultured nation; yet they readily acquiesced in the barbarities designed into the *Barbarossa* plan. These included the starvation of at least 30 million Russians, in order that their food supplies might be diverted to Germany, originally a conception of Nazi agriculture chief Herbert Backe.

Industrialised savagery was inherent in *Barbarossa*. Goering told those charged with administering the occupied territories: 'God knows, you are not sent out there to work for the welfare of the people in your charge, but to get the utmost out of them, so that the German people can live.' From June 1941 onwards, few German senior officers could credibly deny complicity in the crimes of Nazism.

The Soviet Union on the eve of the German invasion was the most rigorously regulated and policed society in the world. Its machinery of domestic repression was much more elaborate, and in 1941 had killed far more people, than that of Nazism: six million peasants perished in the course of Stalin's programme of enforced industrialisation, and vast numbers of loyal comrades had fallen victim to his paranoia. Yet Stalin's tyranny was less prepared to defend itself against foreign enemies than against its own people. The Red Army's formations in the west were poorly deployed, in a thin forward line. Many of its best commanders had been killed in the 1937-38 Purges, and replaced by incompetent lackeys. Communications were crippled by lack of radios and technical skills; most units lacked modern arms and equipment. The dead hand of the Party crippled efficiency, initiative and tactical prudence.

Stalin dismissed many warnings from his own generals as well as from

London about the impending invasion. He also rejected explicit intelligence about *Barbarossa* from Soviet agents in Berlin and Tokyo, scrawling across one such report from Beria: 'You can tell your "source" from the German Air Headquarters that he can go and fuck his mother... I.St.'

Himself a warlord of icy purpose, Stalin was confounded by the apparent perversity of Hitler's behaviour. Under the terms of the Nazi-Soviet Pact, Germany was receiving enormous material aid from Russia; supply trains continued to roll west until the very moment of the invasion; the Luftwaffe's aircraft were largely fuelled by Soviet oil; the Kriegsmarine's U-boats had access to Russian port facilities. Britain remained undefeated. Stalin thus refused to believe that Hitler would precipitate a cataclysmic breach with him, and was personally responsible for the fact that the German onslaught, no surprise to his senior commanders, caught the defences unprepared.

On the western front, some 2.5 million of Stalin's 4.7 million active soldiers were deployed – 140 divisions and forty brigades with more than 10,000 tanks and 8,000 aircraft. Hitler launched against them 3.6 million Axis troops, the largest invasion force in European history, with 3,600 tanks and 2,700 aircraft of superior quality to those of the Russians. The Germans struck from East Prussia into Lithuania, from Poland towards Minsk and Kiev, from Hungary into the Ukraine. Almost everywhere, they smashed contemptuously through Soviet formations, destroying planes wholesale on the ground – 1,200 in the first twenty-four hours.

In the Baltic republics, the invaders were bewildered to be greeted as liberators, with offerings of flowers and food. Latvians seized three towns from their Soviet occupiers before the Germans arrived; by the end of 1941 Estonian partisans claimed to have captured 26,000 Soviet troops. In the Ukraine likewise, the Red Army suffered at the hands of local guerrillas as well as the Germans. The Germans' arrival prompted widespread celebration among Ukrainians on both sides of the Soviet border.

In the first weeks of *Barbarossa*, the Wehrmacht achieved some of the greatest victories in the annals of war. Entire armies were enveloped and destroyed. In brilliant sunshine, German troops in shirtsleeves rode their tanks and trucks in triumphant dusty columns across hundreds of miles of plains, swamps, forests.

The advancing armies streamed through towns and cities reduced to flaming desolation either by their own guns or by the retreating Soviets. Thousands of casualties overwhelmed Russian field hospitals, arriving in trucks or carts, 'some even crawling on their hands and knees, covered in blood', in the words of medical orderly Vera Yukina.

The ruthlessness of the invaders was swiftly revealed. In France in 1940, more than a million French prisoners were caged and fed; in Russia, by contrast, prisoners were caged only to perish. First in hundreds of thousands, soon in millions, they starved to death in accordance with their captors' design. Some prisoners resorted to cannibalism.

Berlin was indifferent. Hitler sought to conquer as much land, and to inherit as few people, as his armies could contrive. He often cited the precedent of the 19th century American frontier, where the native inhabitants were almost extinguished to make way for settlers. On 25 June Police General Walter Stahlecker led Einsatzgruppe A into Kaunas, the Lithuanian capital, behind the panzers. A thousand Jews were rounded up and clubbed to death by Lithuanian collaborators at Lietukis garage, less than 200 yards from Army HQ.

Stalin would ultimately prove the most successful warlord of the conflict, yet no more than Hitler, Churchill or Roosevelt was he qualified to direct vast military operations. Ignorant of the concept of defence in depth, he rejected strategic retreat. Instead he responded to reports of mass surrenders and desertions with draconian sanctions. In the course of the war, a total of around 300,000 Russian soldiers are believed to have been killed by their own commanders for alleged cowardice and desertion – more than the entire toll of British troops who perished at enemy hands in the course of the war.

A critical strand in the Soviet Union's response to *Barbarossa* was a commitment to the doctrine of total mobilisation. It is hard to exaggerate the magnitude of the eastward evacuation of key factories and workers to the Volga, the Urals, Siberia and Soviet Central Asia; the fortitude of those who carried it out; and the importance of its success. Russia's industrial migration eventually embraced 1,523 undertakings including 1,360 major plants. Some 16.5 million workers embarked on new lives in conditions of appalling privation, labouring 11 hours a day, six days a week, initially often under open skies. It is hard to imagine that British or American workers could have established and operated production lines under such handicaps.

Stalin could justly claim that his enforced industrialisation of the Soviet Union in the 1930s, at the cost of imposing misery and death on millions of dispossessed peasants, alone made it possible for the country now to build the tanks and planes to resist Hitler.

In western Russia, meanwhile, the invaders' juggernaut still rolled forward, sustaining complacency in Berlin. Hitler busied himself with detailed planning for his new empire: all dissent was to be rewarded by death. As early as 31 July, Goering ordered preparations for a 'total solution to the Jewish question in the German sphere of influence in Europe'. Tens of thousands of

Russian Jews were slaughtered where they were found, by the Einsatzgruppen killing squads which followed the Wehrmacht's spearheads.

Since the 1917 Revolution, the population of the Soviet Union had endured the horrors of civil war, famine, oppression, enforced migration and summary injustice. But *Barbarossa* transcended them all in the absolute human catastrophe which unfolded in its wake, and eventually became responsible for the deaths of 27 million of Stalin's people, of which 16 million were civilians. A soldier named Vasilii Slesarev received a letter, carried to the Soviet lines by partisans, from his 12-year-old daughter Manya in their home village near Smolensk: 'Papa, our Valik died and is in the graveyard... Papa, the German monsters set fire to us.' The Russians lost 20 casualties for every German, six tanks for every panzer.

By September, Moscow was tantalisingly close. Six German armies – 1.9 million men – participated in Hitler's Operation *Typhoon*, the 'decisive' assault on the capital. Once more the Russians suffered vast losses: eight Soviet armies reeled in the path of the offensive, many units broke, many more were cut off. Major Ivan Shabalin wrote in his diary on 13 October, a few days before his death: 'It is wet and cold and we are moving terribly slowly – all our vehicles are bogged down on the muddy roads...'

Yet the mud Ivan Shabalin complained of was already proving more dangerous to the Germans, as they struggled to advance, than to the defenders holding their ground. Autumn rains were part of Russia's natural cycle, but they astonished the commanders of the all-conquering Wehrmacht.

On 30 October, panzer commander Col. Gen. Erich Hoepner wrote despairingly: 'The roads have become quagmires – everything has come to a halt. Our tanks cannot move.' He added: 'Dear God, give us fourteen days of frost. Then we will surround Moscow!' Hoepner got his weather wish soon enough – far more than 14 days of frost. But the descent of sub-zero temperatures and heavy snow did nothing for the Wehrmacht, and much for its enemies. German vehicle and weapon lubricant froze, and soon likewise soldiers.

The second week of October 1941 was afterwards identified as the decisive period of the crisis. Gen. Zhukov was summoned to the Kremlin; he found Stalin ailing with flu, standing before a map of the front, complaining bitterly about a lack of reliable information. Much of the bureaucracy of Stalin's government had been evacuated from Moscow to Kuibyshev, 500 miles east on the Volga. The dictator himself was about to quit the capital.

Suddenly, however, he changed his mind. He stayed, and declared Moscow a fortress. Order on the streets was restored by a curfew and imposition of the usual brutal sanctions. On 7 November, by a brilliant propaganda stroke, units en route to the front were diverted to stage the traditional parade through the capital celebrating the anniversary of the Bolshevik Revolution. That night came the first heavy snowfall of the year. The Germans, their operations crippled by the weather, lacked sufficient mass to make the final breakthrough; they languished outside the city, suffering rapidly increasing privations.

By the end of November, the German advance had exhausted itself. 'The Führer himself has taken charge,' wrote Kurt Grumann, 'but our troops walk around as if they were doomed.'

In Berlin on 28 November, a conference of industrialists chaired by armaments supremo Fritz Todt reached a devastating conclusion: the war against Russia was no longer winnable. Having failed to achieve a quick victory, Germany lacked resources to prevail in a sustained struggle. For the rest of the war, those responsible for Germany's economic and industrial planning did so in the knowledge that strategic success was unattainable. Whatever the prowess of the Wehrmacht, the nation lacked means to win; it could aspire only to force its enemies to parley, together or severally. Gen. Alfred Jodl, the Führer's closest and most loyal military adviser, asserted in 1945 that his master understood in December 1941 that 'victory could no longer be achieved'.

CHAPTER FIVE

MOSCOW SAVED, LENINGRAD STARVED

Even as the fate of Russia's capital was decided, further west a parallel drama unfolded, of almost equal magnitude and embracing even greater human suffering. From north-west and south, in the autumn of 1941 Axis forces closed upon Russia's old capital Leningrad. *Barbarossa* persuaded the Finns (invaded by Russia in 1940) to avenge their defeat. On 15 September, with their aid, the Germans completed the encirclement of Leningrad. The ensuing siege of the city – the tsars' St. Petersburg with its elegant avenues, baroque palaces and seaside quays – became an epic which continued for more than two years. It assumed a character unique in its horror, and cost its defenders and citizens more lives than Britain and America together lost in the entire war.

Before the battle began, Soviet commanders had anticipated a direct assault. Zhukov, dispatched from Moscow to take charge of Leningrad's defence, placed blocking units – *zagradotryady* – behind the front, to shoot down his own men who attempted to flee, a practice which became institutionalised in the Red Army. German propaganda loudspeakers taunted their doomed assailants on the battlefield: 'It's time to assemble at your extermination points again – we shall bury you on the banks of the Neva.' Then the next barrage fell

EUROPE 1942

NORWAY

SWEDEN

DENMARK

IRELAND

GREAT
BRITAIN

NETHERLANDS

London ●

Berlin ●

BELGIUM

GERMANY

BOHEMIA
MORAVIA

Atlantic Ocean

● Paris

FRANCE

VICHY

SWITZERLAND

ITALY

PORTUGAL

SPAIN

Rome ●

Mediterranean Sea

SIC

upon Soviet troops milling helpless in their positions.

For weeks, the Russians remained oblivious of the fact that the Germans had no intention of launching a ground attack on Leningrad, nor even of accepting its surrender. Hitler, instead, set out to starve the city to death. Professor Ernst Zigelemeyer of Munich's Institute of Nutrition – one of many scientists who provided satanic counsel to the Nazis – agreed that no battle was necessary; it would be impossible for the Russians to provide their beleaguered citizens with more than 250 grams of bread a day, which could not sustain human life on a protracted basis: 'It is not worth risking the lives of our troops. The Leningraders will die anyway.'

The first major Luftwaffe attack on Leningrad destroyed the waterside Badaev warehouses, holding most of the city's food stocks; melted sugar ran along a neighbouring road, and fires burned for days. The citizens quickly understood their plight. A woman named Elena Skryabina wrote in her diary: 'We have returned to prehistoric times. Life has been reduced to one thing – the hunt for food.' Every vestige of vacant soil was tilled for vegetables, each plot marked with its owner's name. The bread ration fell below the level the murderous Professor Zigelemeyer deemed necessary for existence. Pigeons vanished from the city squares as they were caught and eaten, as too were crows, gulls, then rats and household pets.

By December 1941, the outside temperature had dropped to -30 degrees celsius, and starvation was killing thousands. Yet the privileged escaped most of the suffering. For the dignitaries who stayed in Leningrad, bread, sugar, meatballs and other cooked food remained readily available at a canteen in the Smolny Institute, with access to a private heated cinema.

But while Russians were dying in their thousands as 1941 drew to a close, two million German soldiers, their tunics lined with newspaper and straw to compensate for the clothing they lacked, were in straits almost as dire as those of Russia's people. Between 22 June 1941 and 31 January 1942, Germany suffered almost a million casualties, more than a quarter of all the soldiers originally committed to *Barbarossa*.

The deeper within the country heavy fighting took place, the graver became the logistical difficulties of supplying Hitler's troops, with few railways and inadequate numbers of trucks, which themselves consumed precious fuel merely to deliver loads. The key battles of the 1940 French campaign took place within a few hours' drive of the German border; now the Wehrmacht was committed to a struggle thousands of miles from its bases.

Stalin's personal direction of Russia's 1941 campaigns inflicted disasters which at times threatened to become irretrievable; his refusal to yield ground was responsible for the loss of many of the 3.35 million Russian soldiers who passed into German captivity that year. But his people revealed a will to fight, and a willingness to die, which owed little to ideology and much to peasant virtues, a visceral devotion to Mother Russia, and the fruits of compulsion.

To discourage desertion, the Red Army adopted a new tactic: dispatching groups of men towards the German lines with their hands in the air, who then tossed a shower of grenades; this was designed to provoke the Germans to fire on others who attempted to surrender in earnest.

The ruthlessness of the Soviet state was indispensable to confound Hitler. No democracy could have established as icily rational a hierarchy of need as did Stalin, whereby soldiers received most food; civilian workers less; and 'useless mouths', including the old, only a starvation quota: more than two million Russians died of starvation during the war in territories controlled by their own government. The Soviet achievement in 1941-42 contrasted dramatically with the feeble performance of the Western Allies in France in 1940; whatever the limitations of the Red Army's weapons, training, tactics and commanders, Soviet culture armoured its forces to meet the Wehrmacht with a resolution the softer citizens of the democracies could not match.

It was probably true that only Russians could have borne and achieved what they did in the face of the 1941 catastrophe. But even when Russia became joined with the democracies to achieve the defeat of Nazism, Stalin pursued his quest for a Soviet empire, domination and oppression of hundreds of millions of people, with absolute single-mindedness and ultimate success. Whatever the merits of the Russian people's struggle to expel the invaders from their country, his war aims were as selfish and inimical to human liberty as those of Hitler. Soviet conduct could be deemed less barbaric than that of the Nazis only because it embraced no single enormity to match the Holocaust. Nonetheless, the Western Allies were obliged to declare their gratitude, because Russia's suffering and sacrifice saved the lives of hundreds of thousands of young British and American soldiers. Even if no exalted assertion of principle – instead, only a breach between rival monsters – caused Russia to become the principal battleground of the war, it was there that the Third Reich encountered the forces that would contrive its nemesis.

CHAPTER SIX

AMERICA EMBATTLED

The people of the United States observed the first 27 months of the struggle in Europe with mingled fascination, horror and disdain. Many saw the conflict, and the triumphs of Nazism, as reflecting a collective European degeneracy. There was limited animosity towards the Axis, and some active support for Hitler in German ethnic communities. Very few wanted to see their own nation join either side in a bloodbath an ocean apart from their own continent.

For half the previous decade, President Franklin Roosevelt had been expressing dismay about his people's reluctance to acknowledge their own peril. Given the strength of isolationism, however, between 1939 and 1941 he felt obliged to act with circumspection in aiding Britain.

The writer John Steinbeck spent some weeks in the spring of 1940 sailing down the Pacific coast of South America, from whence he wrote to a friend: 'We haven't heard any news of Europe since we left and don't much want to.' Like many liberals, Steinbeck was convinced America would eventually have to fight, but viewed the prospect without enthusiasm.

Many intellectuals disdained Europe's war because they perceived it as a struggle between rival imperialisms. They recoiled from association with the preservation of the British, and for that matter French and Dutch, empires; they questioned whether a war fought in harness with old Tories could be dignified as a moral undertaking. The treasurer of Harvard, William Claflin, told the university's president: 'Hitler's going to win. Let's be friends with him.' In the September 1940 *Atlantic Monthly*, Kingman Brewster and Spencer Klaw, editors respectively of the Yale and Harvard student papers, published a manifesto asserting students' determination not to save Europe from Hitler.

Roosevelt gained domestic support for both aid to Britain and US rearmament by adopting the argument advanced by Gen. John Pershing, his nation's most famous soldier of World War I: his policies would not hasten engagement in the conflict, but instead push it away from America's shores. The British were obliged to pay cash on the nail for every weapon shipped to them until their cash and gold reserves were exhausted, and Lend-Lease kicked in, late in 1941. It was as a defensive measure that Roosevelt reconciled the American people to the September 1940 destroyers-for-bases deal with Britain, which even the isolationist *Chicago Tribune* welcomed: 'Any arrangement which gives the US naval and air bases in regions which must be brought within the American defense zone is to be accepted as a triumph.'

Though Winston Churchill strained every sinew to induce the US president to lead his nation into belligerence before Pearl Harbor, it was fortunate that his efforts failed: in the unlikely event that Roosevelt could have forced a declaration of war on Germany through the US Congress, thereafter he would have led a divided nation. Until December 1941, public opinion remained stubbornly opposed to fighting Hitler.

Even after war was declared in December 1941, and indeed until the end of hostilities, few Americans felt anything like the animosity towards Germans that they displayed against the Japanese. This was not merely a matter of racial sentiment; there was also passionate sympathy for the horrors China had experienced, and continued to experience, at Japanese hands. Most Americans deplored what the Nazis were doing to the world, but would have remained unenthusiastic or indeed implacably hostile about sending armies to Europe, had not Hitler forced the issue.

Japan's military leaders made their critical commitment in 1937, when they embarked upon the conquest of China. This provoked widespread international hostility, and proved a strategic error of the first magnitude; amid the vastness of the country, their military successes and seizures of territory were meaningless. A despairing Japanese soldier scrawled on the wall of a wrecked building:

> Fighting and death everywhere and now I am also wounded. China is limitless and we are like drops of water in an ocean. There is no purpose in this war. I shall never see my home again.

Though the Japanese dominated the China war against the corrupt regime

and ill-equipped armies of Generalissimo Chiang Kai-shek, they suffered debilitating attrition. Even a huge deployment of manpower – a million Japanese soldiers remained in China until 1945 – proved unable to force a decisive outcome upon either Chiang's Nationalists or the communists of Mao Zedong, whose forces they confronted and sometimes engaged across a front of 2,000 miles.

Western perceptions of the war with Japan are dominated by the Pacific and south-east Asian campaigns. Yet China, and Tokyo's refusal to abandon its ambitions there, were central to Japan's ultimate failure. Its withdrawal from the mainland could probably have averted war with the United States, since Japanese aggression there, and the culture of massacre symbolised by the deaths of at least 60,000 and perhaps many more civilians in Nanjing, was the principal source of American animosity, indeed outrage. Moreover, even if China's own armies were ineffectual, Japan's commitment imposed a massive haemmorhage of resources. The curse upon the Tokyo government was its dominance by soldiers committed to the perceived virtue of making war for its own sake: intoxicated by a belief in their warrior virility, they failed to grasp the difficulty, even impossibility, of successfully making war upon the United States, the world's greatest industrial power, impregnable to assault.

On 27 September 1940, the Tripartite Pact signed in Tokyo between Germany, Italy and Japan, promised mutual assistance if any of the parties was attacked by a nation not engaged in the European war. This was a move designed to deter the United States from exerting further pressure on Japan, and it failed. The US, implacably hostile to Japanese imperialism in China, imposed further sanctions. In response, the Japanese committed themselves to execute the 'strike south' strategy. They prepared to seize the West's ill-defended south-east possessions in a series of lightning operations, bludgeoning America into acquiescence by evicting its forces from the western Pacific.

In the middle of 1941, the Japanese military drafted their optimistically titled 'Operational Plan for ending the war with the US, Britain, the Netherlands and Chiang Kai-shek'. With the notable exceptions of a few such enlightened officers as Admiral Isoroku Yamamoto, naval commander-in-chief, Japanese regarded Americans as an unwarlike and frankly degenerate people, whom a series of devastating blows would reconcile to a negotiated peace.

The calculations of Japan's militarists were rooted in conceit, fatalism – a belief in *shikata ga nai*, 'it cannot be helped' – and ignorance of the world outside Asia. Japan's soldiers had remarkable powers of physical endurance, matched by willingness for sacrifice, but the army was seriously deficient in tanks and artillery; the country's industrial and scientific base was much too weak to support a sustained conflict against the US. Germany and Japan never seriously co-ordinated strategy or objectives, partly because they had few in common beyond defeat of the Allies, and partly because they were geographically remote from each other. Hitler's racial principles caused him to recoil from association with the Japanese, and only grudgingly to acknowledge them as his co-belligerents.

Japan launched its strike against Pearl Harbor and assault on south-east Asia on 7 December 1941, just 24 hours after the Russians began the counter-offensive which saved Moscow.

The nakedness of America's Pacific bases continues to puzzle posterity. Overwhelming evidence of Tokyo's intentions was available throughout November, chiefly through decrypted diplomatic traffic; in Washington as in London, there was uncertainty only about Japanese objectives. The thesis advanced by extreme conspiracists, that President Roosevelt chose to permit Pearl Harbor to be surprised, is rejected as absurd by all serious historians. It remains nonetheless extraordinary that his government and chief of staffs failed to ensure that Hawaii, as well as other bases closer to Japan, were on a full precautionary footing. On 27 November 1941, Washington cabled all Pacific bases: 'This dispatch is to be considered a war warning. An aggressive move by Japan is expected within the next few days... Execute appropriate defensive deployment.' The failure of local commanders to act effectively in response to this message was egregious; at Pearl Harbor on 7 December, anti-aircraft ammunition boxes were still locked, their keys held by duty officers.

But it was a conspicuous feature of the war that again and again, dramatic changes of circumstance unmanned the victims of assault. Senior commanders, never mind humble subordinates, found it hard to adjust their mindset and behaviour to the din of battle until this was thrust upon them, until bombardment became a reality rather than a mere prospect. Admiral Husband Kimmel and Lt. Gen. Walter Short, respectively navy and army commanders at Pearl Harbor, were unquestionably negligent; but their conduct reflected an institutional failure of imagination which extended up the entire US command chain to the White House, and inflicted a trauma on the American people.

'We were flabbergasted by the devastation,' wrote a sailor aboard the carrier *Enterprise*, which entered Pearl Harbor late on the afternoon of 8 December, having been mercifully absent when the Japanese struck. 'One battleship, the *Nevada*, was lying athwart the narrow entrance channel, beached bow first, allowing barely enough room for the carrier to squeeze by... The water was covered with oil, fires were burning still, ships were resting on the bottom mud, superstructures had broken and fallen.'

The assault on Pearl Harbor prompted rejoicing throughout the Axis nations. Japanese lieutenant Izumiya Tatsuro wrote exultantly of 'the glorious news of the air attack on Hawaii'. Mussolini, with his accustomed paucity of judgement, was delighted: he thought Americans stupid, and the United States 'a country of Negroes and Jews', as did Hitler. Yet fortunately for the Allied cause, American vulnerability on Hawaii was matched by a Japanese timidity which would become an astonishingly familiar phenomenon of the Pacific conflict. The core reality was that the Pearl Harbor attack sufficed to shock, maul and enrage the Americans, but not to cripple their war-fighting capability. It was thus a grossly misconceived operation.

Hitler had always expected to fight Roosevelt's people once he had completed the destruction of Russia; in December 1941, he considered it a matter of course to follow Japan's lead, and entertained extravagant hopes that Hirohito's fleet would crush the US Navy. Four days after Pearl Harbor, he made the folly of the strike comprehensive by declaring war on the United States, relieving Roosevelt from a serious uncertainty about whether Congress would agree to fight Germany.

The struggle would cost the United States less than any other combatant; indeed, it generated an economic boom which enabled Americans to emerge from the war much richer than they started. But for all the exuberant declarations of patriotism that followed the 'Day of Infamy', many Americans remained resentful about the need to accept even a modest share of the privations thrust upon most of the world's peoples.

Fortunately for the Allied cause, however, the leadership of the United States showed itself in this supreme crisis both strong and wise. At Roosevelt's Washington summit with Churchill at the end of December 1941, the US confirmed its provisional commitment, made during earlier staff talks, to prioritise war with Germany.

The US chiefs of staff recognised that Germany represented by far the more dangerous menace; the Japanese, for all their impressive frontline military and naval capability, could not threaten the American or British homelands. Nonetheless, it was plain to the governments of Britain and America, if not to their peoples, that a long delay was in prospect before Western land forces could engage Germany on the continent. For years to come, Russia must bear the chief burden of fighting the Wehrmacht. And as long as the Eastern Front remained the decisive ground theatre, aid to Russia was a priority.

Meanwhile, in the East, Japan held the initiative, and deployed formidable forces on land, at sea and in the air. Having devastated the battleships of the US Pacific Fleet, the Japanese now fulfilled their longstanding ambition to

WAR IN THE PACIFIC
US torpedo bombers on the USS
Enterprise *during the Battle of
Midway, June 1942*

seize the American dependency of the Philippines, together with the vast
natural resources of the Dutch East Indies – modern Indonesia – British Hong
Kong, Malaya and Burma. Within the space of five months, against feeble
resistance, they created an empire. Even though this would prove the most
short-lived in history, for a season Japan gained dominance of vast expanses
of the Asian landmass and Pacific seascape.

CHAPTER SEVEN

JAPAN'S SEASON OF TRIUMPH

Many Japanese welcomed the war, which they believed offered their country its only honourable escape from beleaguerment. Novelist Dazai Osamu, for instance, was 'itching to beat the bestial, insensitive Americans to a pulp'. But Japan's 1941-42 successes against feeble western resistance caused both sides to overrate the power of Hirohito's nation. Just as Germany was not strong enough to defeat the Soviet Union, Japan was too weak to sustain its Asian conquests unless the West chose to acquiesce in early defeats.

Until December 1941, the sluggish, humid, pampered rhythm of colonial life in Asia was scarcely interrupted by events in Europe. In Malaya, Britain's military commanders and rulers alike reflected paucity of talent: the empire seemed to have an inexhaustible supply of unwarlike warrior chieftains. Sir Shenton Thomas, the colony's governor, said to the generals as the Japanese began to land in the north early on 8 December: 'I suppose you'll shove the little men off.'

The Japanese could exploit almost absolute command of sea and air. When Gen. Tomoyuki Yamashita's forces met stubborn resistance at Kampar in central Malaya, he simply launched a new amphibious landing to outflank the defenders. The cultural chasm between foes was exposed when British troops surrendered. They expected the mercy customarily offered by European armies, even those of the Nazis; instead, they were stunned to see their captors killing casualties incapable of walking, often also unwounded men and civilians. The teenage daughter of a Chinese teacher who brought food to an Argyll officer in his jungle hiding place one day left a note in English for him about the Japanese: 'They took my father and cut off his head. I will continue to feed you as long as I can.'

From the outset, fleeing British clung to the racial conventions of empire and shamelessly abandoned their native subjects. When Penang island was evacuated, for example, non-Europeans were denied access to shipping. The behaviour of British communities in Malaya and later Burma was rational enough: word had reached south-east Asia about the orgy of rape and massacre which accompanied the fall of Hong Kong to the Japanese at the end of December. But the spectacle of white rulers succumbing to panic mocked the myth of benign imperial paternalism.

On 31 January 1942, the causeway linking Malaya to Singapore Island was blown up. Yamashita's forces began landing on Singapore Island in darkness on 8 February, employing a makeshift armada of 150 boats which carried 4,000 men in the first wave, two divisions in all. Shellfire quickly severed most phone communications in forward areas, and heavy rain left sodden defenders huddled in their trenches.

Churchill dispatched a histrionic signal to General Wavell, newly-appointed Allied supreme commander, urging a last-ditch resistance in Singapore:

> The battle must be fought to the bitter end at all costs... Commanders and senior officers should die with their troops. The honour of the British Empire and of the British Army is at stake.

Churchill's message is important. He demanded from Singapore's garrison no more and no less grit and will for sacrifice than Germans, Japanese and Russians routinely displayed, albeit under threat of draconian sanctions. Even if Malaya was lost, the prime minister sought to salvage some redeeming legend, of its defenders resisting to the last. But the concept of self-immolation was beyond the bounds of Western democratic culture.

Lt. Gen. Arthur Percival surrendered Singapore to Yamashita on 15 February. The photograph of a British officer named Major Wylde, in baggy shorts and helmet askew beside his general as they carried the Union flag to the Japanese lines, became one of the defining images of the war. It seemed to symbolise the bungling, blimpish ineffectuality of the men who had been entrusted with defence of Britain's eastern Empire. Along with Singapore,

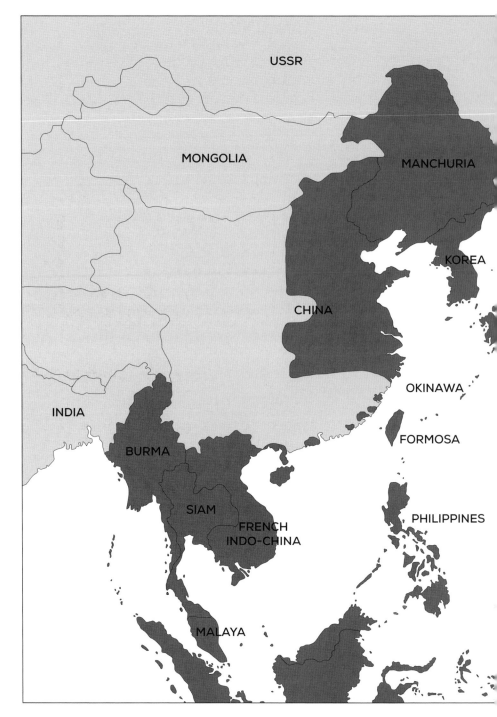

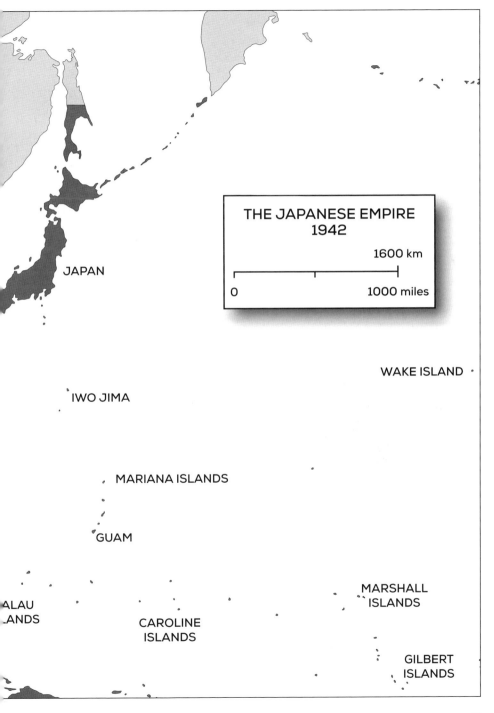

THE JAPANESE EMPIRE
1942

1600 km

0   1000 miles

JAPAN

WAKE ISLAND

IWO JIMA

MARIANA ISLANDS

GUAM

PALAU
ISLANDS

CAROLINE
ISLANDS

MARSHALL
ISLANDS

GILBERT
ISLANDS

Percival signed away a significant portion of the honour of the British and Indian Armies, as Churchill and his people well understood. The Japanese had gained their victory in barely 70 days, at a cost of only 3,506 dead. Yamashita and his officers celebrated victory with dried cuttlefish, chestnuts and wine, gifts of the emperor, set out upon a white tablecloth.

It has sometimes been asserted that Yamashita's post-war execution for war crimes was unjustified, but the general was never even indicted for the systematic massacres of Chinese which took place at Singapore under his command. Yamashita once delivered a speech in which he asserted that, while his own people were descended from Gods, Europeans were descended from monkeys. British racism in south-east Asia was now eclipsed by that of the Japanese. Tokyo's new regime was characterised by a brutality such as the evicted imperialists, whatever their shortcomings, had never displayed.

The Japanese began their treatment of Allied prisoners as they intended to continue. After the fall of Hong Kong on Christmas Day 1941, the invaders launched an orgy of rape and massacre which embraced nuns and nurses, hospital patients bayoneted in their beds. Similar scenes took place on Java and Sumatra, largest islands of the Dutch East Indies, which were easily overrun after the fall of Singapore. The Japanese Army in its new conquests sustained the tradition of savagery which it had established in China, a perversion of virility and warrior spirit which was the more shocking for being institutionalised.

The conquerors, emboldened by their Malayan triumph, seized the opportunity also to occupy British Burma, partly to secure its oil and natural resources, partly to close the 'Burma Road' to China. This was not a disaster of the same magnitude as Malaya, and Gen. Bill Slim conducted his retreat with some skill. But the Japanese now occupied Britain's entire south-east Asian empire, to the gates of India. The loss of Britain's empire in south-east Asia brought disgrace as well as defeat on its rulers, as Winston Churchill readily recognised.

After Pearl Harbor, America's political and military leaders knew that they, like the British, must suffer defeats and humiliations before forces could be mobilised to roll back the advancing Japanese. Remarkably, within a mere seven months of Pearl Harbor American fleets had gained victories which turned the tide of the Asian war – including the decisive victory near Midway atoll. The US navy soon showed itself the most impressive of the nation's fighting services, and at Midway it inflicted devastating damage on the Japanese fleet. While Germany dominated Western Europe for four years, by autumn 1942 the Japanese perimeter was already beginning to shrink. The speed of the American resurgence in the Pacific reflected the fundamental weakness of the Asian enemy.

First, however, came the pain. In the Philippines, the Japanese advanced on Manila against negligible resistance. In Washington, the US chiefs of staff wisely forswore any notion of reinforcing the defence. Gen. Douglas MacArthur enjoyed just one piece of good fortune: the invaders focused on occupying the capital, and made no attempt to frustrate his retreat to the peninsula of Bataan.

The four-month defence of Bataan and Corregidor in early 1942, which cost 2,000 American dead, was made possible in part by Japanese incompetence. But nothing can detract from the gallantry of Gen. Wainwright, who directed the defence, and of his garrison. They created a legend in which Americans could take pride – and of which Churchill was envious. To put the matter bluntly, US soldiers on Bataan and Corregidor showed themselves more stalwart than British imperial forces in Malaya and at Singapore, albeit likewise in a doomed cause.

Gen. MacArthur, meanwhile, had escaped to Australia by PT-boat in obedience to an order from Roosevelt. Brigadier Dwight Eisenhower, who had served unhappily under MacArthur a few years earlier, wrote in his diary: 'Poor Wainwright! He did the fighting... [MacArthur] got such glory as the public could find... MacArthur's tirades, to which... I so often listened in Manila... would now sound as silly to the public as they then did to us. But he's a hero! Yah.'

Eisenhower, however, failed to grasp the importance of legends, indeed myths, to sustain the spirit of nations in adversity. The epic of Bataan and MacArthur forged by Roosevelt and the US media was serviceable, even precious to the American people. The general was a vainglorious windbag rather than a notable commander, whose personality was repugnant. But his flight from Corregidor was no more discreditable than those of many wartime British commanders from stricken fields, including Wavell's from Singapore. During the years that followed, MacArthur's status as a figurehead for American endeavours in the south-west Pacific did much for morale at home, if less for the defeat of Japan.

It is remarkable that, once Tokyo's hopes of quick victory were confounded and American resolve had been amply demonstrated, Hirohito's nation simply fought blindly on. But no more in Japan than in Germany did any faction display will and power to deflect the country from its march towards immolation. *Shikata ga nai*: it could not be helped. If this was a monumentally inadequate excuse for condemning millions to death without hope of securing any redemptive benefit, it is a constant of history that nations which start wars find it very hard to stop them.

CHAPTER EIGHT

THE BRITISH AT SEA

O nce Hitler had achieved mastery of the European continent in 1940, the British Army's part in the struggle against Nazism became subordinate or even marginal, and remained so until 1944. Beyond Britain's symbolic role in holding aloft the standard of resistance to Hitler, its principal strategic importance became that of a giant aircraft-carrier and naval base, from which the bomber offensive and return to the continent were launched. It fell to the Royal Navy to conduct the critical struggles of 1940-43 to keep the British people fed, to hold open the sea lanes to the Empire and overseas battlefields, and convoy munitions to Russia. Naval might could not bring about the defeat of Germany. But if German efforts to interdict shipments to Britain were successful, Churchill's people would starve.

In the first war years, surface raiders imposed as many difficulties as U-boats. German sorties between 1939 and 1943 precipitated dramas which seized the attention of the world: the pocket-battleship *Graf Spee* sank nine merchant-men before being scuttled after its encounter with three British cruisers off the River Plate in December 1939. The 56,000 ton *Bismarck* destroyed the battlecruiser *Hood* before being somewhat clumsily dispatched by converging British squadrons on 27 May 1941.

The Atlantic was the dominant naval battlefield, forever the cruel sea. And while Germany's capital ships commanded headlines, Axis submarine and air forces represented a much graver long-term threat, and the men of both arms displayed courage and skill.

In the course of 1941, 3.6 million tons of British shipping were lost, 2.1 million of these to submarines. Churchill became deeply alarmed; his postwar assertion that the U-boats caused him greater anxiety than any other threat to Britain's survival has powerfully influenced the historiography of the war. It is scarcely surprising that the prime minister was so troubled, when almost every week until May 1943 he received loss statistics that represented a shocking drain on British transport capabilities.

But just as the Luftwaffe in 1940-41 attempted to deal a knockout blow to Britain with wholly inadequate resources, so the U-boat arm lacked strength to accomplish the severance of the Atlantic link. Germany never built anything like enough submarines to make them a war-winning weapon.

It is a remarkable and important statistic, that 99% of all ships which sailed from North America to Britain during the war years arrived safely. Yet, as is the way of mankind, the Allies perceived most of the difficulties on their own side. Churchill and Roosevelt saw only a steeply rising graph of losses which, if it had continued exponentially, would have crippled the war effort. And while the German offensive was mismanaged, especially in 1941-42 Allied merchant seamen suffered grievously from its consequences.

Even those fortunate enough to survive a sinking often faced terrible ordeals in open lifeboats. But there were many examples of heroic endeavour, such as that of the 10,350-ton diesel cargo-liner *Otari*. On 13 December 1940, 450 miles west of the British coast homeward bound from Australia, she was hit by a torpedo, causing the sea to rush into her after-holds. Frozen sheep carcases and cases of butter were soon bobbing in the ship's wake; *Otari*'s propeller shafts were leaking, and the engine-room bulkhead threatened to collapse. But Captain Rice, her master, decided she might be saved: alone on the ocean, mercifully shrouded by mist from further enemy mauling, for three days he and his crew patiently coaxed the *Otari* onward, her pumps just sufficing to sustain buoyancy. The ship at last reached the mouth of the Clyde in darkness, to find that its defensive boom was closed. Only at dawn on 17 December was Rice finally able to bring his ship, decks almost awash, into the anchorage; most of its precious cargo was salvaged by lighters. By such stubborn determination and courage was Britain's Atlantic lifeline held open.

When Hitler invaded Russia, the British and American chiefs of staff alike opposed the dispatch of military aid, on the grounds that their own nations' resources were too straitened to spare arms for others. Britain's prime minister and America's president overruled these objections, asserting – surely rightly – that support for the Soviet war effort was an absolute priority.

The experiences of the 'PQ' convoys, as they were codenamed, became one of the war's naval epics. Even before the Germans entered the story, Arctic weather was a terrible foe: ships often found themselves ploughing through mountainous seas, while laden with a top weight of hundreds of tons of ice. Crews were obliged to labour relentlessly, hacking dangerous weights of ice

LIVING WITH WAR

The war meant very different things to different people. Some found that bearing their share of their nations' struggle for conquest or freedom rendered sorrows tolerable, ennobled loneliness and danger. But the humbler their personal circumstances, the slighter seemed the compensations for sacrifice. William Crawford, a 17-year-old boy second class serving aboard the battlecruiser *Hood*, wrote home miserably:

> Dearest Mum... I know it's wrong to say but I sure am fed up. I feel kind of sick, I can'nae eat and my heart's in my mouth. We struck bad weather today. Talk about waves as big as houses, they're crashing over our bows... I wonder if it would do any good Mum if you wrote to the Admiralty and asked them if there was no chance of me getting a shore job at Rosyth. You know, tell them you have got two sons away and that. Be sure to tell them my age. If only I could get off this ship it would not be so bad.

Crawford, however, was still aboard *Hood* when she was sunk with almost all hands in May 1941.
Only a small number of warriors articulated hopes more ambitious than those for personal survival. One of these was a British officer who wrote to his parents before being killed in his first North African battle:

> I should like you to know what it is I died for... There is, I feel, both in England and America a tremendous

surge of feeling, a feeling which, for want of a better word, I shall call 'goodness'... It is the heartfelt longing of all the 'middling folk' for something better – a world more worthy of their children, a world more simple in its beliefs, nearer to earth and to God.

All this was true. While Winston Churchill saw himself conducting a struggle to preserve the greatness of the British Empire, most of his fellow-countrymen yearned instead for domestic change, most vividly anticipated in the Beveridge Report, published in November 1942, which laid the foundations of Britain's postwar Welfare State.
Isolation was a towering sensation, even for men serving amid legions of their compatriots. Although soldiers often talk about women, under the stress and unyielding discomfort of a battlefield most crave simple pleasures, among which sex scarcely features. A US Marine Corps lieutenant-colonel in the south Pacific fantasised about his ambitions on returning home:

> I'm going to start wearing pyjamas again... I'm going to polish off a few eggs and several quarts of milk... A few hot baths are also in order... But I'm saving the best for last – I'm going to spend a whole day flushing a toilet, just to hear the water run.

Countless families struggled to come to terms with loss. British army officer's wife Diana Hopkinson described a reunion with her from upperworks and guns, testing weapons on which lubricants froze. Lt. Alec Dennis, first lieutenant of a destroyer, tried to nap on deck because he knew that if he took to his bunk he would be pitched out. He spent the first hour of every four off-watch thawing his frozen feet sufficiently to be able to sleep.

AFTER DUNKIRK
A woman from the Mechanised Transport Corps hands out tea to returning soldiers

husband on a station platform in Berkshire, after a long separation during which they received news that his brother had been killed in action:

His strange uniform, his strangely thin face glimpsed in the dimmest light, gave me a feeling of artificiality. Even in our kisses there was something unreal. In bed there was a terrible sadness to overcome – Pat's death – before we could make love. When at last he turned towards me, we made

love as if we were partners in a solemn rite, strange, speechless, but familiar.

Sheffield housewife Edie Rutherford was just preparing tea when her young neighbour, wife of an RAF pilot, knocked on the door.

Her face was wooden and she jerked out: 'Mrs. Rutherford, Henry is missing', thrust the telegram into my hand. Of course I just opened my arms and took her in and let her have a good weep while I cursed audibly this blasted war.

Merchant ships crawled across the chill sea more slowly than a running man, exposed to bomb and torpedo assaults more deadly than those of the Atlantic campaign. Yet Churchill angrily rejected the Royal Navy's urgings to suspend convoy operations during the perpetual daylight of Arctic summer. And the human cost of the PQs was astonishingly small, by the standards of other battlefields; though 18 warships and 87 merchantmen were lost, only 1,944 naval personnel and 829 merchant seamen died serving on Arctic convoys between 1941 and 1945. Given Germany's extraordinary opportunities for strategic dominance of the Arctic in 1942, what is remarkable is not how many Allied ships they sunk, but how few.

CHAPTER NINE

OUT OF AFRICA

A t the outbreak of war in 1939, Hitler had no intention of waging war in the Mediterranean, and asserted his determination not to commit German resources there. It was his fellow dictator Benito Mussolini who on his own initiative launched the offensives which brought conflict to the region. In the year after the fall of France in June 1940, only in the African and Balkan theatres did Allied and Axis armies clash; even after Germany invaded Russia in June 1941, the Mediterranean remained for three more years the focus of the Western Allied military contribution to the struggle against Hitler. All this was the consequence of Mussolini's decision to become a protagonist in a struggle for which his nation was pitifully ill-equipped.

Hitler possessed in the Wehrmacht a formidable instrument for fulfilling his ambitions. 'Il Duce' (as Mussolini was known) sought, by contrast, to play the warlord with incompetent commanders, unwilling soldiers and inadequate weapons. Italy was relatively poor, with a GDP less than half the size of Britain's. Even in the sunshine days of Mussolini's relationship with Hitler, such was the Nazis' contempt for their ally that 350,000 Italian workers in Germany were treated little better than slaves. In 1936, when a foolish woman at a party asked Field-Marshal Werner von Blomberg who would win the next war, he is alleged to have answered: 'Madam, I cannot tell you that. Only one thing I can say: whoever has Italy on his side is bound to lose.'

Ashore, in North Africa, the clashes between desert armies were little more significant in determining the outcome of the global conflict than the

THE DESERT FOX
Rommel in Africa in June 1942

tournaments between bands of French and English knights which provided *entre'actes* during the Hundred Years' War. But the North African contest caught the imagination of the western world, and achieved immense symbolic significance in the minds of the British people. It became what will surely prove to have been history's last campaign fought overseas between European powers attempting to advance European objectives.

The men who fought the desert war suffered fewer hardships than those serving in Russia, Burma or the Pacific, but water shortage imposed chronic discomfort. 'The flies plague us in millions from the first hour in the morning,' wrote an Italian officer. 'The sand always seems to be in our mouths, in our hair and in our clothes, and it is impossible to get cool.' In tanks, the temperature often rose above 50 degrees celsius. Opening hatches merely allowed sand and dust to swirl in.

Neither Churchill nor his people doubted the importance of the struggle in Russia, but North African operations mattered much to British self-respect. Following the ignominious surrender of Tobruk in Libya on 21 June 1942, Gen. Sir Claude Auchinleck took personal charge of Eighth Army. But at the end of the month, beaten at Mersa Matruh, his battered formations retreated yet again, to the El Alamein line inside Egypt.

British fortunes were then at their lowest ebb. Morale was wretched. It seemed plausible to both sides that Rommel might reach Cairo. The strategic impact of such a blow would have been limited. But the cost to British prestige, already badly tarnished, would have been appalling. Panic swept Egypt, and the Royal Navy's Mediterranean Fleet quit Alexandria.

Yet the British predicament was not as bad as they themselves supposed. The RAF in North Africa was gaining strength, while the Luftwaffe had been weakened. Whatever delusions Rommel's soldiers cherished, his army lacked strength to make a final push for Alexandria with a realistic prospect of success. Vanity and ambition often caused 'the Desert Fox' to overreach himself, and Hitler urged ill-judged aggression upon the Afrika Korps even more insistently than Churchill pressed his own commanders.

Auchinleck was well-placed to frustrate Axis purposes, merely by holding his ground. American and British forces were to land at the opposite end of North Africa in November – Operation *Torch* – and this made it unnecessary for Eighth Army to take risks. Once the Allies established themselves in Morocco, Algeria and Tunisia, Rommel's position in Egypt would become untenable. But as autumn approached, the success of *Torch* seemed ill-assured, especially in Washington. For the British, there was also the imperative of national prestige: since 1939 Churchill's armies had suffered repeated defeats

– indeed humiliations. Spirits at home were low. A British victory was desperately needed. The defeat of the Afrika Korps in Egypt had become an issue of the highest moral importance.

In the first days of August Churchill arrived in Cairo with Alan Brooke, his military advisor, to see for himself. He sacked Auchinleck, who was replaced as Eighth Army commander by Brooke's nominee, Lt. Gen. Sir Bernard Montgomery, and as Middle East C-in-C by Gen. Sir Harold Alexander. A month later, on 30 August, Rommel attacked at Alam Halfa. Montgomery, provided by Ultra with full details of German plans, drove him back. The general then addressed himself to training Britain's troops for his own offensive.

The volume of Ultra intelligence was now increasing exponentially, with critical influence in every theatre. In 1940, after the capture of a German Enigma machine, the British Code and Cypher School at Bletchley Park had begun to break German and Italian messages, and from mid-1942 onwards, with a few important breaks, the Allies became privy to much of their enemies' signal traffic. The penetration of German and Japanese ciphers made a massive contribution to victory. Beyond the achievements of British and American decrypters, it was a secondary miracle that the Axis powers never seriously suspected that their most secret communications were being accessed by the enemy.

In the autumn of 1942, Churchill was passionately impatient for Eighth Army to attack. Once the *Torch* landings took place, the glory of every subsequent British success would be shared with the Americans. Alexander and Montgomery were relentlessly chivvied from London, though the foxy little field commander stuck to his own timetable. A cold, incisive, self-consciously professional soldier, 'Monty' was determined to impose on British operations an order and discipline which had hitherto been absent; his most conspicuous attribute was 'grip'. Between August and October 1942, in a remarkable fashion he revived the confidence of the desert army.

Keith Douglas, traversing the rear areas of Eighth Army to join an armoured regiment, was fascinated by the spectacle of men and machines massing in the sands for battle: 'Lorries appeared like ships, plunging their bows into drifts of dust and rearing up suddenly over crests like waves... Every man had a white mask of dust in which, if he wore no goggles, his eyes showed like a clown's eyes.' On 23 October, Montgomery launched Operation *Lightfoot*, the opening phase of the 12-day second Alamein battle, which began with a devastating bombardment. Men choking amid the acrid fumes of explosions watched tongues of flame leaping up across the desert.

For almost a week, repeated British attacks were beaten back. In London,

Churchill fumed. Then the picture changed, dramatically. Attrition imposed intolerable losses on the Axis forces, whose fuel shortage had become acute. Rommel, returning from sick leave to the battlefield, signalled Berlin that he was embarking upon a full-scale retreat, revealed by Ultra to the triumphant British; by 4 November, Eighth Army was advancing in pursuit across open desert, while Axis units sought escape.

Eighth Army's armoured units sped westward, their tracks churning sand, their crews thrilled that months of deadlock were broken. 'The view from a moving tank is like that in... a silent film,' wrote Keith Douglas, 'in that since the engine drowns all other noises except explosions, the whole world moves silently.' On and on they drove, through heavy rain. Montgomery's caution prevented them from converting success into destruction of Rommel's army, but the British had achieved the only substantial land victory of the Western war for which they shared laurels with no ally.

The *Torch* landings in Vichy French Algeria and Morocco on 8 November 1942 represented the first big combined operation against the Germans by the US and British armies. The North African advances thrilled the peoples of the Allied nations, once they dared to believe that these were more than mere swings of the pendulum. Muriel Green, by now one of Britain's 80,000 'land girls' providing agricultural labour, scribbled on 11 November: 'Suddenly realized the news has become exciting... I really think things are beginning to happen and that victory is on the way.' But while Churchill ordered the church bells of Britain rung for victory in North Africa, much more pain and hardship lay ahead before the Allies would enjoy real cause for celebration.

CHAPTER TEN

THE BEAR TURNS: RUSSIA IN 1943

A t midsummer 1942, the western Allies' view of Russia's predicament remained bleak. A British intelligence officer wrote on 15 July: 'I have the inescapable feeling that much as the Germans may have lost, the Red Army has lost more.' By now, though, as posterity knows, Stalin had learned vital lessons. Profiting from experience as Hitler would not, he delegated operational control of the battlefield; such a drastic step was indispensable, to remedy the Red Army's lamentable summer performance.

In the autumn and winter of 1942, the grey, charmless industrial city of Stalingrad became the scene of some of the most terrible fighting of the war. On Sunday, 23 August, the Germans heralded their assault with an air raid by 600 aircraft: 40,000 civilians are said to have died in the first 14 hours, almost as many as perished in the entire 1940-41 blitz on Britain. Thereafter, the Luftwaffe struck relentlessly. 'It is incomprehensible to me how people can continue to live in that hell,' wrote Stuka pilot Herbert Pabst.

The Russians fought for Stalingrad with a desperation reinforced, as always, by compulsion. The price of unauthorised retreat was death. Some 13,500 soldiers were executed at Stalingrad for alleged cowardice or desertion, and many more were killed out of hand. Stalin's orders were simple and readily understood: the city must be held to the last man and woman.

It was Hitler's ill-fortune that the battle perfectly suited the elemental spirit of the Red Army. A panzer grenadier officer wrote:

EASTERN FRONT
*Citizens of Leningrad during
the 872-day siege*

We have fought for fifteen days for a single house, with mortars, machine-guns, grenades and bayonets. The front is a corridor between burnt-out rooms… The street is no longer measured in metres, but in corpses. Stalingrad is no longer a town. By day it is an enormous cloud of burning, blinding smoke; it is a vast furnace lit by the reflection of the flames. And when night arrives – one of those scorching, howling, bleeding nights – the dogs plunge into the Volga and swim desperately for the other bank. The nights in Stalingrad are a terror for them. Animals flee this hell… only men endure.

Strategically, the northern struggle, where fighting continued unabated along hundreds of miles of front, was much less important than the battle for Stalingrad. Nonetheless, Leningrad's experience was at least as significant, in showing why the Soviet Union prevailed in the Second World War. It is unthinkable that British people would have eaten each other rather than surrender London or Birmingham – or would have been obliged by their generals and politicians to hold out at such a cost. If Leningrad's inhabitants had been offered an exchange of surrender for food in February 1942, they would assuredly have given up. But in the Soviet Union no such choice was available, and those who attempted to make it were shot. Both Hitler and Stalin displayed obsessive stubbornness about Leningrad; that of Stalin was finally rewarded, amid a mountain of corpses. A people who could endure such things displayed qualities the Western Allies lacked, which were indispensable to the destruction of Nazism. In the auction of cruelty and sacrifice, the Soviet dictator proved the higher bidder.

Even as the defenders of Leningrad were experiencing a fragile revival of life and hope, further east and south the Stavka, Russia's high command, launched its strategic counter-strikes. Operation *Mars*, which began on 25 November 1942, cost 100,000 Russian lives, and was repulsed. But in January 1943 the German line in the east suffered a succession of crippling blows. On the 12th, in the far north, the Stavka launched an attack which, at the end of five days' fighting, opened a corridor along the shore of Lake Ladoga that broke the siege of Leningrad. In late January, Soviet forces closed on Rostov, threatening German forces in the Caucasus. On 31 January, General Paulus surrendered the remains of Sixth Army at Stalingrad.

Soviet generalship sometimes displayed brilliance, but mass remained the key element in the Red Army's stunning successes in early 1943. The fundamental cause of the disasters which befell the German armies was that they had undertaken a task beyond their nation's powers. Meanwhile, the superiority of Stalin's armies had grown alongside the confidence of his generals. Soaring weapons output increased the Red Army's advantage: the Russians were building over 1,200 T-34s a month, while the Germans produced only 5,976 Panthers and 1,354 Tigers, their best tanks, during the whole war.

In June 1943, by scraping together reinforcements, Hitler was able to deploy in Russia just over three million German troops. He acknowledged that a general offensive remained impracticable, but insisted on a single massive thrust. His attention focused upon a bulge in the Soviet front west of a mono-syllabic place name that would enter the legend of warfare: Kursk.

From the outset, each side recognised Kursk as a titanic clash of forces and wills; Stuka dive-bombers and SS Tiger tanks inflicted heavy losses on Russian T-34s; many of the new German Panthers were halted by breakdowns, but others forged on, crushing Soviet anti-tank guns in their path, while panz-ergrenadiers grappled Gen. Zhukov's infantry, using flame-throwers against trenches and bunkers. Both sides' artillery fired almost without interruption.

In the great melee of armour, some tanks of the rival armies collided, halting in a tangle of tortured steel; there were many exchanges of fire at point-blank range. Across hundreds of miles of dusty plain and blackened wreckage, the largest armoured forces the world had ever seen lunged at each other, twisting and swerving. The important reality was that German losses were unsustain-able. Two thousand miles away, as the battle began, the six US and British divisions which had landed in Sicily began to sweep across the island.

Hitler's nerve broke. On 13 July, he told his generals he must divert two SS Panzer divisions to strengthen the defence of Italy. The German army sustained a tigerish defence in the Kursk salient until 25 July, then started to fall back. A month later the Russians regained Kharkov. Soldier Alexander Slesarev wrote to his father: 'We're crossing liberated territory… People emerge joyfully to greet us, bringing apples, pears, tomatoes, cucumbers…" But the resumption of Soviet rule was not an unmixed blessing for Stalin's people. The Germans had permitted peasants to sow and harvest their own plots; the returning Soviets reimposed rigorous collectivisation, which provoked some protest riots. Every tractor and almost every horse was gone, so that land could be tilled only with spades and rakes, sometimes by women pulling ploughs. Even sickles were seldom available.

The Germans staged their initial withdrawal from Kursk in good order, though no one on either side doubted that they had suffered a calamitous defeat, sustaining half a million casualties in 50 days of fighting. Over half the Soviet territory lost to Hitler since 1941 had been regained.

CHAPTER ELEVEN

DIVIDED EMPIRES

Most of the nations which escaped involvement in World War Two were protected by geographical remoteness. Turkey was the most significant state to sustain neutrality, having learned its lesson from rash involvement in World War One on the side of the Central Powers. In Europe, only Ireland, Spain, Portugal, Sweden and Switzerland were fortunate enough to have their sovereignty respected by the belligerents, most for pragmatic reasons.

The Atlantic 'air gap' was significantly widened, and many lives and much tonnage lost, in consequence of the fanatical loathing of Irish prime minister Eamonn de Valera for his British neighbours. Almost every warship and merchantman that sailed past the Irish coastline in the war years felt a surge of bitterness towards the country which relied on Britain for most of its vital commodities and all its fuel, but would not lift a finger to help in its hour of need. 'The cost in men and ships... ran up a score which Irish eyes a-smiling on the day of Allied victory were not going to cancel,' wrote corvette officer Nicholas Monsarrat.

The Swedes asserted their neutral status with a rigour promoted by proximity to Germany, arresting and imprisoning scores of Allied intelligence agents and informants. Switzerland was a hub of Allied intelligence operations, though the Swiss authorities foreclosed all covert activities they discovered. They also denied sanctuary to Jews fleeing the Nazis, and profited enormously from pocketing funds deposited in Swiss banks by both prominent Nazis and their Jewish victims, which later went unclaimed because the owners perished.

SINGAPORE FALLS
General Arthur Percival, led by a Japanese officer, walks under a flag of truce to negotiate the capitulation of Allied forces on 15 February 1942

Switzerland also provided important technological and industrial support for the Axis war effort. The war proved good for business in the ice-hearted cantons.

Much more complex and brutal issues of loyalty confronted societies occupied by the Axis, or subject to colonial rule by the European powers. French gendarmes consigned Jews to death camps (although, despite the legend of Dutch sympathy promoted by Anne Frank's diary, Holland's policemen proved even more ruthless than their French counterparts, dispatching a higher proportion of their country's Jews to deportation and death). Everywhere Vichy held sway, the French treated captured Allied servicemen and civilian internees with callousness, and sometimes brutality.

In mainland France, the Resistance enjoyed support from only a small minority of people until the Germans' 1943 introduction of forced labour persuaded many young men to flee to join maquis groups, for which they afterwards fought with varying degrees of enthusiasm. To challenge the occupiers was difficult and highly dangerous. Given the strong French tradition of anti-semitism, there was little appetite for assisting Jews to escape the death camps. Much of France's aristocracy collaborated with the Germans, as well as with the Vichy regime which governed central and southern France until the Germans took them over in November 1942.

Elsewhere, some small countries showed bolder defiance than did the French. The Danes, alone among European societies, refused to participate in the deportation of their Jews, almost all of whom survived. Further east, large numbers of Ukrainians and citizens of the Baltic states enlisted in the Wehrmacht, disliking Stalin's Soviet Union more than the Nazis. Ukrainians provided many of the guards for Hitler's death camps.

Britain's Asian empire manifested the most conspicuously divided allegiances. Many people in Burma, Malaya and the Dutch East Indies at first welcomed the invading Japanese as liberators. Even ardent foes of European imperialism were soon disillusioned, however, by the arrogance and institutionalised brutality of their new masters. Examples are legion: far more local people died as slaves on the notorious Burma Railway than did Allied prisoners. Of almost 80,000 Malays sent to work there, nearly 30,000 perished, alongside 14,000 whites; the rail link also cost the lives of 100,000 Burmese, Indians and Chinese.

British-occupied India, as nationalists regarded the sub-continent, experienced bitter wartime upheavals and distress. The Indian Army remained almost entirely staunch. But all save the most myopic British imperialists recognised that their rule had lost the consent of the governed. It was a source of embarrassment to thoughtful politicians that in 1942, in the midst of a war against tyranny, some fifty battalions of troops – more than were then

JAPAN AND BIOLOGICAL WEAPONS

All estimates are unreliable, but it seems reasonable to accept the figure of 15 million Chinese wartime dead as a direct consequence of Japanese military action, starvation or plagues, some of these deliberately fostered by biological warfare specialists of the imperial army's Unit 731.

The Japanese were the only large-scale wartime users of biological weapons. Unit 731 in Manchuria operated under the supremely cynical cover name of The Kwantung Army Epidemic Protection and Water Supply Unit. Thousands of captive Chinese were murdered in the course of tests at 731's base near Harbin, many being subjected to vivisection without benefit of anaesthetics. Some victims were tied to stakes before anthrax bombs were detonated around them. Women were laboratory-infected with syphilis; local civilians were abducted and injected with fatal viruses. In the course of Japan's war in China, cholera, dysentery, plague and typhus germs were broadcast, most often from the air, sometimes using porcelain bombs to deliver plague fleas.

That the Japanese attempted to kill millions of people with biological weapons is not seriously questioned; it is less certain, however, how successful were their efforts. Yet even if Japan's genocidal accomplishments fell sort of the sponsors' hopes, the nation's moral responsibility is manifest.

committed against the Japanese – had to be deployed to maintain internal control of India.

Americans, from their president downwards, never entirely forgave Churchill and his nation for the manner in which the peoples of the sub-continent were excluded from the ringing promises of freedom enshrined in the Atlantic Charter. But while Americans serving in India believed their own behaviour more sympathetic, Indians were less convinced, and the British saw hypocrisy as well as moral conceit in criticism of their imperial governance by an ally which sustained racial segregation at home in the United States.

Most of Churchill's political colleagues recognised the inevitability of granting early independence to India, and hesitated only about timing. But the old Victorian imperialist remained implacable: he clung to a delusion that British greatness derived in substantial measure from the Raj, and was disgusted by the perceived treachery of Indian politicians who sought to exploit Britain's vulnerability and sometimes rejoiced in its misfortunes. Throughout the war, the prime minister spoke and wrote about Indians with a contempt that reflected his only aquaintance with them, as a nineteenth-century subaltern; his policies lacked the compassion which generally characterised his leadership.

By the autumn of 1942 more than 30,000 of India's Congressmen were imprisoned, including Congress leader Jawaharlal Nehru and Mahatma Gandhi. But British treatment of dissenters throughout their empire was incomparably more humane than that accorded by the Axis to domestic foes and occupied nations. For instance, Captain Anwar Sadat, who later became Egypt's president, was jailed after being implicated in a conspiracy with German spies in Cairo, but so casually guarded that he was able to make two easy escapes; after the second, in 1944, he remained free, though in hiding, for the rest of the war. In India, Nehru could write letters freely, enjoy such favourite books as Plato's *Republic* and play badminton during a relatively privileged fortress incarceration. But his weight fell dramatically, and confinement bore down heavily upon the fifty-two-year-old Indian leader as on any other prisoner. In one letter, he told his wife Betty to abandon the notion of sending him Bradley's *Shakespearean Tragedy* 'when there is tragedy enough at present'.

The common experience of battle forged some sense of battlefield comradeship between British and imperial soldiers white, brown and black alike. But the stress of war, rather than strengthening the bonds of empire as Britain's jingoes liked to pretend, dramatically loosened them.

CHAPTER TWELVE

ITALY: HIGH HOPES, SOUR FRUITS

The Western Allied armies, by deferring a major landing on the continent until 1944, restricted themselves to a marginal role. The Russians eventually killed more than four and a half million German soldiers, while American and British ground and air forces killed only about 500,000. These figures emphasise the disparity between respective military contributions.

For Churchill's and Roosevelt's soldiers to have played a decisive role in the ground battle against Germany, they would have needed to land on the European continent at least 40 divisions, and probably more, in 1943 before the Russians achieved their great victories. These armies did not exist. Equally important, shipping was lacking to transport such a force to the continent and keep it supplied thereafter. The Luftwaffe remained relatively potent: its nemesis came in the following year, at the hands of the USAAF's Mustang fighters over Germany. Allied dominance of French air space, which proved absolute in 1944, would have been contested had the Allies landed earlier.

The Americans were willing to risk landing a small army in France in 1943. The British, who would have had to provide most of the men, were not. They judged, almost certainly rightly, that unless they deployed overwhelming strength they would suffer another disaster, as painful as those of the early war years. Even if a continental campaign in 1943 had proved sustainable, it would

have cost hundreds of thousands more casualties than the Anglo-American armies suffered in 1944-45, since it would have faced German forces much stronger than those which the Allies met on and after D-Day, following a further year of attrition on the Eastern Front.

Finding it impossible to launch a grand ground commitment in Europe in 1943, the British and Americans instead opted for limited operations against the Axis southern flank. Churchill and his generals, who pushed for this, were thus far right, that it was essential to attack the Italian mainland, the only battlefield where Anglo-American ground forces could engage the Germans. But they underestimated the difficulties of advancing through mountainous territory against a skilful and stubborn defence.

The campaign, which began in Sicily, taught the Anglo-Americans painful lessons. Amphibious and related air operations were poorly planned and clumsily managed. Co-ordination between air and ground forces was lacking. If Italian troops had fought with the same determination as the Germans, the invaders would have been pushed back into the sea. The Americans were dismayed by General Alexander's lack of grip, contemptuous of Montgomery's sluggishness, irked by their ally's apparent desire to relegate them to a subordinate role. The British, in their turn, were exasperated by the reluctance of American commanders, especially General Patton, to conform to agreed plans. The Germans executed masterly ambushes and demolitions, a foretaste of their tactics up the length of Italy during the next two years. The invaders failed to exploit sea power to outflank resistance, and merely conducted a succession of slogging matches.

British and American troops began to land on the coast of Sicily on 10 July, 1943. Two weeks later, in Rome, King Victor Emmanuel and Marshal Pietro Badoglio contrived the arrest of Mussolini. Europe's first fascist leader scarcely protested his own downfall. His spirit was broken, he was resigned to defeat and seemed chiefly concerned to save his own skin. The ex-Duce spent the ensuing weeks of captivity, first on offshore islands then at a ski resort in the Apennines, eating prodigious quantities of grapes, reading a life of Christ and attending mass for the first time since childhood. (It is doubtful that he much relished his later rescue by Otto Skorzeny's Nazi commandos. Though restored to puppet power in northern Italy, he knew that his game was played out.)

On 8 September, five days after the Allies began their assault on the Italian mainland, Marshal Badoglio's government announced Italy's surrender, prompting renewed optimism about a swift advance up the peninsula. Instead (and though the new Italian government declared war on Germany in October), the stage was set for 18 months of slow and costly fighting in some of the most unyielding country in Europe. After days or weeks of attrition, the Germans made a measured withdrawal to a new mountain or river line, protected by demolition of bridges, rail links and access roads. Everything of value to the civilian population as well as to the Allies was pillaged or destroyed. It was estimated that 92% of all sheep and cattle in southern Italy together with 86% of poultry were taken or killed by the retreating army. With the malice that so often characterised German behaviour, General Kesselring's men destroyed much of Naples's cultural heritage before abandoning the city, burning whole mediaeval libraries, including the university's 50,000 volumes.

An American likened fighting in Italy to 'climbing a ladder with an opponent stamping on his hands at every rung'. For the Allies, there was an iron imperative to renew the assault. Captain Henry Waskow, a 25-year-old Texan, led his diminished company on a night attack against one of innumerable German mountain positions, known only as Hill 730, on the moonlit night of 14 December 1943. 'Wouldn't this be an awful spot to get killed and freeze on the mountain?' he murmured wryly to his runner. He felt a sudden yearning for toast. 'When we get back to the States, I'm going to get me one of those smart-aleck toasters where you put the bread in and it pops up.' A few seconds later, he was mortally wounded by a shell fragment when the Germans spotted the advancing Americans. Waskow left behind a letter for his family, of a kind which many young men penned:

I would like to have lived. But, since God has willed otherwise, do not grieve too much, dear ones, for life in the other world must be beautiful, and I have lived a life with that in mind all along… I will have done my share to make the world a better place…

It was only because many young men of many nations shared Waskow's dogged commitment to do 'the right thing', as each belligerent society defined this, that the war could be carried on.

The principal victims of the campaign were the people of Italy. If Benito Mussolini had preserved Italian neutrality in 1940, it is possible that he might have sustained his dictatorship for many years in the same fashion as General Franco of Spain, who presided over more mass murders than the Duce, yet was eventually welcomed into membership of NATO. It is unlikely that Hitler would have invaded Italy merely because Mussolini clung to non-belligerent status; the country had nothing Nazi Germany valued except views.

The Germans, having previously regarded their Italian Allies as mere poltroons, now viewed them as traitors, and acted ruthlessly against partisans. The most notorious massacre of innocents was carried out under the direction of Rome's Gestapo chief, Lt. Col. Herbert Kappler. On 23 March 1944, partisans attacked a marching column of the Bozen Police Regiment in the Via Rasella. Gunfire and explosives killed 33 Germans and wounded 68, while ten civilians were also killed. In reprisal, Hitler demanded the deaths of ten Italians for each German. Next afternoon, 335 prisoners were taken from the Regina Coeli prison to the Ardeatine Caves. They were a random miscellany of actors, lawyers, doctors, shopkeepers, cabinet-makers, an opera singer and a priest. Some were communists, and 75 were Jews.

Two hundred of them had been seized in the streets near the Villa Rasella following the partisan attack, though none were involved in it. In batches of five, they were led into the caves, executed, the bodies left where they fell. Though the Germans used explosives to close the shaft in a half-hearted attempt to conceal the massacre, this was rendered inffectual by the stench that soon seeped forth. The caves became a place of pilgrimage and tears.

It is bizarre that General Kesselring, under whose orders the Gestapo acted, escaped execution at Nuremburg.

CHAPTER THIRTEEN

WAR IN THE SKY

Young men of all nations perceived romance in playing their parts in the war as knights of the air. It was ironic, therefore, that many such dreamers found themselves instead committed to aerial bombardment of cities, one of the more barbarous features of the conflict.

Allied aircrew, once deployed on operational fighter or bomber squadrons, until the last 18 months of the war confronted a statistical probability of their own extinction. Romantic delusions faded, as they learned to anticipate a destiny as a bloody jam of crushed flesh and bones, or surmounting a petrol-fuelled funeral pyre. To be sure, their daily lives on the ground were privileged; they were spared the mud and discomfort to which foot soldiers were subjected. But they were less likely to survive. Ernie Pyle, the great American correspondent, wrote: 'A man approached death rather decently in the air force. He died well-fed and clean-shaven.'

More than half the RAF's heavy bomber crews perished, 56,000 men in all. The USAAF's overall losses were lower, but among 100,000 of its men who participated in the strategic offensive against Germany some 26,000 died. 'You were resigned to dying every night,' said a British Whitley bomber pilot, Sid Bufton. 'Before setting out you looked around your room: golf clubs, books, nice little radio – and the letter to your parents propped up on the table.'

Throughout 1940-41, naïveté persisted within the RAF about the effectiveness of Bomber Command's operations. 'We thought we were knocking hell out of them,' said Ken Owen, a 19-year-old navigator. 'There

THE LUFTWAFFE
German bombers over Poland

was a tremendous amount of self-delusion. Maybe 12 times [out of 30 "trips"] I think we bombed the right place; otherwise it was either the wrong place or ploughed fields.'

But despite the limited impact of the strategic air offensive in its early years, it suited not only the air chiefs, but also Britain's prime minister and America's president, to collude in proclaiming the triumphs of bombing. Sir Arthur Harris, who became Bomber Command's C-in-C in February 1942, said: 'Winston's attitude to bombing was "anything to put up a show".'

Until 1943, the most important achievement of the Allies' strategic air offensive was that it obliged the Germans to divert growing numbers of their fighters and dual-purpose 88mm guns from the Eastern Front to defence of the Reich. Richard Overy argues convincingly that the German war effort suffered severely from the need to commit resources to home defence. The Luftwaffe was obliged to divert almost its entire 1943-45 fighter strength to Germany, conceding almost total air superiority over both Eastern and Western battlefields to the Allies. It is also plain that, while Albert Speer contrived to increase output even amid the massive air attacks of 1944, vastly more weapons would have been built if factory operations had been unimpeded.

The outstanding precision bombing feat of the war was the RAF's May 1943 attack on the Ruhr dams, an epic of ingenuity, skill and courage, though its economic significance was modest. As early as 1937, the Air Ministry identified Germany's water supply as a key factor in steel production, and in 1940 Chief of Air Staff Sir Charles Portal urged an attack on reservoirs. The difficulty was to find appropriate means. Scientist and aircraft-designer Barnes Wallis was independently pursuing the same purpose, and conceived the notion of bouncing depth-charges against dam walls. In February 1943, his project won official backing, despite the scepticism of Sir Arthur Harris. Wallis was asked to produce the weapons in time for an attack in May, when the Ruhr reservoirs would be full. Initial tests were carried out with a spherical charge, but in April Wallis determined upon a cylindrical alternative, backspun before release by an electrically-driven pulley so that it would 'crawl' down a dam wall to detonate 33 feet below the water surface. Astonishingly, in barely a month the four-ton weapons were built, and Lancasters specially modified to carry them.

The specially formed 617 Squadron trained throughout April and early May to carry out the attack. Contrary to popular myth, not every man was a volunteer, nor were all crews highly experienced. This makes all the more remarkable the achievement of 24-year-old Wing-Commander Guy Gibson, a fierce disciplinarian and obsessively dedicated airman, in preparing his unit to launch the attack on the night of Sunday 16 May. Nineteen crews took off. The Mohne and Eder dams were identified as priority targets.

The Mohne was breached by the fourth weapon dropped, the Eder by the third and last available to the attacking Lancasters. Eight crews failed to return, a punitive casualty rate: six of them fell victims to anti-aircraft fire during the deck-level flights to and from the Ruhr in bright moonlight, indispensable to bombing accuracy.

The destruction of the Mohne and Eder created a sensation, and won the admiration of the world. The moral impact of the attack was enormous, not least on Germany's leaders, and much enhanced the prestige of Bomber Command; Gibson received a VC. The loss of water imposed only temporary inconvenience upon Ruhr steel production, but if the economic impact of 'the Dambusters' raid' was limited, the propaganda achievement was great. All those involved richly merited their laurels.

In 1943, the German economy staggered amid the combined pressures of shortages of coal, steel and manpower; this was the first year in which the air offensive inflicted massive damage on the Nazi war machine. Bombing did not make the decisive impact upon civilian morale which the British aspired to achieve. But the misery of urban Germans became very great; the Nazi regime was driven to increasingly desperate expedients to explain to its own people their vulnerability to air assault. Newspaper headlines after the May 1943 dams raid asserted that it was 'the work of Jews'. The public was unconvinced: security police reported that many citizens merely asked why the Luftwaffe was incapable of such achievements.

As bombing intensified and civilian morale slumped, oppression and compulsion were employed ever more ruthlessly to sustain Nazi hegemony. In 1943, the courts passed a hundred death sentences a week on citizens deemed guilty of defeatism or sabotage. To maintain output, the aircraft industry adopted a 72-hour working week, and, as slave labour became increasingly important, General Erhard Milch urged ever more draconian measures to increase its productivity. He wrote of foreign and PoW workers: *'International law cannot be observed here... I have very strongly represented the point of view that prisoners, with the exception of the English and the Americans, should be taken away from the military authorities... If [a prisoner of war] has committed sabotage or refused to work, I will have him hanged, right in his own factory.'*

Though the RAF inflicted huge damage on Germany, it was left to the USAAF to achieve the most important victory of the air war, in the early months of 1944, by means which surprised its own commanders. The USAAF embarked on a major campaign against aircraft factories, pounding them for six consecutive days of 'Big Week' in February, and forcing the Luftwaffe to commit every available fighter to their defence. It quickly became plain that destruction achieved by the bombers on the ground was less significant than the startling success of American pilots in air combat. In a single month, the Luftwaffe lost one-third of its fighters and one-fifth of its aircrew. When D-Day came in June, Goering's shrunken squadrons were unable to offer significant support to the Wehrmacht.

The inhabitants of Germany's cities experienced a scale of terror and devastation far beyond anything the Luftwaffe inflicted on Britain in 1940-41: a successful bomber attack unleashed a vision of hell. More than a few Germans, and even some Anglo-American critics, see a moral equivalence between Nazi wickedness in massacring innocents, especially Jews, and Allied wickedness in burning cities. This seems mistaken. The bomber offensive was designed to achieve the defeat of the Axis and liberation of Europe. The Nazis' mass murders not only killed far more people, but lacked the justification of pursuing a strategic purpose: instead, they were conducted solely to fulfil Nazi Germany's ideological and racial objectives.

When it was all over, the American and British airmen who had participated in the strategic offensive against Germany, at such risk and sacrifice to themselves, were dismayed to find their campaign the object of criticism and indeed opprobrium. They had bombed the Nazi war economy into a state of collapse; unfortunately, however, their achievement came too late to secure the credit which the air chiefs thought their due: the Allied armies stood on the brink of completing the Reich's defeat by their own exertions. The bomber offensive made a significant contribution to the outcome, but reached its terrible maturity too late to claim success on its own terms.

It is unjust that fighter pilots of all nations today retain a popular adulation often denied to bomber aircrew. Moral strictures upon strategic air attack should properly be deployed against those who instigated it, rather than those who carried it out. The killing of civilians must always be deplored, but Nazi Germany represented an historic evil; until the last day of the war, Hitler's people inflicted appalling sufferings upon the innocent. The destruction of their cities and deaths of significant numbers of their inhabitants seems a price they had to pay for the horrors which they unleashed upon western civilization, and represents a far lighter toll than Germany imposed upon the rest of Europe.

PLANNING THE HOLOCAUST
Reinhard Heydrich (right) with Heinrich Himmler

CHAPTER FOURTEEN

VICTIMS

Hans Frank, Nazi ruler of Poland, wrote in his 1942 diary: 'The power and the certainty of being able to use force without any resistance are the sweetest and most noxious poison that can be introduced into any Government.' In ordinary peacetime life, men and women's actions are constrained not only by law, but by social convention. But the men who exercised authority under the totalitarian regimes, emphatically including that of the Soviet Union, knew themselves liberated from all constraints and safeguards upon the sanctity of human life. This huge, terrible freedom thrilled its beneficiaries.

The edifice of Holocaust literature is vast, yet does not satisfactorily explain why the Nazis accepted the economic cost of embarking upon the destruction of the Jewish people, diverting scarce manpower and transport to a programme of mass murder, while the outcome of the war still hung in the balance. The answer must lie in the deranged centrality of Jewish persecution not merely to National Socialist ideology, but to Germany's policies throughout the global conflict. The Nazis were always determined to exploit the licence granted to a government waging total war to fulfil objectives that otherwise posed difficulties even for a totalitarian regime.

For more than two years after war came, however, the priority of securing victory was held to require postponement of an absolute elimination of European Jewry. Between August 1939 and the summer of 1942, when the death camp programme achieved full capacity, the Nazis contented themselves with killing large numbers of people in many countries on an arbitrary and opportunistic basis.

During these two years, and especially after the invasion of Russia, Germans killed Jews whimsically, on a scale largely determined by availability of manpower and resources. A German ordnance sergeant from a bakery company recalled: 'I saw these people being rounded up and then just had to look away, as they were clubbed to death right before our eyes... A great many German soldiers, as well as Lithuanians, stood there watching. They did not express either assent or disapproval – they just stood, totally indifferent.'

The *Einsatzgruppen* were relatively few and small; they achieved some impressive massacres, notably in the Ukraine, but their victims were still numbered only in tens of thousands. The logistical difficulties of wholesale murder proved immense, even when labour-saving expedients were adopted, such as herding victims into mass graves before shooting them. At such a sluggish pace, the process of 'solving Europe's Jewish problem' would require decades, and in the summer of 1941 SS commanders began to demand a much more radical and comprehensive approach.

Late in July 1941, a new policy was adopted: confinement of east European Jews to ghettos, where they became easier to control and deploy for labour service. The Wehrmacht strongly supported this measure, because it resolved administrative difficulties in its rear areas. The SS extended its range of Jewish murder victims to include many more women and children but, after experiencing the practical difficulties of industrial killing, few SS officers yet felt able to accept a challenge as ambitious as exterminating the entire race.

Final victory in Russia was still assumed to be imminent; until this came, with a consequent liberation of resources, most of the Nazi leadership favoured deferring a 'Final Solution'. Heinrich Himmler, however, was less patient: he saw swift eradication of Jews in the occupied territories both as a national priority and as a means of extending his personal authority. The most powerful fiefdom in Nazi Germany pursued the extinction of the Jews almost heedless of its impact on the country's warmaking. As John Lukacs has observed, Himmler focused far more single-mindedly on this objective than did Hitler.

In September 1941, the Reichsführer SS was given explicit licence to conduct ethnic cleansing in the east. This decision marked the onset of the Third Reich's systemic campaign of genocide. Himmler pursued the extermination of Jews with a concentration of purpose conspicuously absent from every other aspect of Nazi policy-making. Any rational assessment of Germany's predicament in late 1941 demanded dedication to winning the war, above all against the Soviet Union. But Himmler committed the SS to a task which could contribute nothing to German victory, and indeed diverted resources from its achievement.

Through the autumn and into the winter of 1941, the pace of slaughter accelerated: scores of towns and villages were systematically purged of Jews. It seems important to emphasise that, by the time the Final Solution was agreed, at least two million Soviet PoWs had already been killed or allowed to die. All moral barriers to mass murder had been broken down, ample precedent for wholesale killing established, before the major massacres of Jews were ordained.

By December 1941, most Jews in the Baltic states were dead; thousands of collaborators recruited by the Germans as 'local voluntary troops' participated enthusiastically in the killings. For the rest of the war, Latvians, Lithuanians, Estonians and Ukrainians played an important part in Himmler's Jewish extermination programme – over 300,000 were eventually enlisted as auxiliaries to the SS, men who might credibly otherwise have served in Hitler's armies.

The Wehrmacht was wholly complicit in Himmler's operations, even though the SS did most of the killing. General Karl-Heinrich von Stulpnagel on 30 July 1941, for example, cautioned his units not to shoot civilians indiscriminately, but instead to concentrate upon 'Jewish and Communist inhabitants'. The Wehrmacht routinely provided logistical support for SS massacres, together with troops to cordon killing fields. On many documented occasions, army units participated in shootings, despite orders from higher commanders against such sullying of soldierly honour. Without the Wehrmacht's active assistance, mass murder on the scale that took place in 1941-42 would have been impossible. By the end of 1941, at least half a million east European Jews were dead.

The elimination of European Jewry assumed an ever-higher priority on the Nazis' agenda: Hitler convinced himself that the August 1941 Atlantic Charter, together with America's looming entry into the war, derived from Jewish influence on the United States government. This lent a new urgency to his determination to kill their co-religionists in Europe. He came to view this as an objective as important as military victory, and even as a pre-condition for achieving it. Attempts to discern rationality in Nazi strategy, especially from 1941 onwards, founder in the face of such a mindset.

Peter Longerich, one of the more authoritative historians of the Holocaust, has convincingly argued that the Nazi leadership's commitment to executing the Final Solution through designated death camps was not made until the end of 1941: 'The leadership at the centre and the executive organizations on the periphery radicalized one another through a reciprocal process.' Construction of the first purpose-built extermination camp at Belzec near Lublin began only on 1 November 1941. 'In autumn 1941,' writes Longerich, 'the Nazi leadership began to fight the war on all levels as a war "against the Jews".' The construction of gas chambers commenced at Chelmno, Belzec, Auschwitz and elsewhere. Gas trucks had already been employed for the murder of mental patients in Germany and parts of the Nazi empire. Himmler welcomed wider use of such technology, not least to ease the psychological strain which mass shootings imposed on his SS.

A Berliner named Hilde Meikley watched the removal of local Jews: 'Sadly I have to say that many people stood in the doorways voicing their pleasure as the wretched column went by. "Just look at those cheeky Jews!" someone shouted. "They're laughing now, but their last hour has come."' The victims were permitted to carry 50 kilogrammes of baggage apiece. All their valuables were seized at the departure stations, where body searches were conducted and passengers were required to pay fares. Luggage was loaded onto freight wagons, never to be seen again by its owners. Local authorities took possession of vacated housing, which was reallocated to eager new tenants. The rhetoric of Alfred Rosenberg and Goebbels, acknowledging the fact of the deportations to the world, was uncompromising. Rosenberg told a November 1941 press conference:

Some six million Jews still live in the East, and this question can only be solved by a biological extermination of the whole of Jewry in Europe. The Jewish question will only be solved for Germany when the last Jew has left German territory, and for Europe when not a single Jew stands on the European continent as far as the Urals.

So many prominent Nazis spoke explicitly and publicly about their intentions towards the Jews that it remains remarkable that the Allied national leaderships were so reluctant to accept their words at face value. Helmuth von Moltke of the Abwehr informed the British by secret letter via Stockholm in March 1943: 'At least nine-tenths of the [German] population do not know that we have killed hundreds of thousands of Jews... If you told these people what has really happened they would answer: you are just a victim of British propaganda.'

Within some Allied nations, there was equivalence, or worse, in defining attitudes to the greatest of all Nazi persecutions. Anti-semitism was etched deep into Russian history and attitudes, and the revelation of the death camps posed a dilemma for Moscow, which the Soviet authorities never entirely resolved. They could not applaud the Nazis' slaughter of the Jews, but to acknowledge its enormity was to require a sharing of the Russian people's overpowering sense of victimhood, which they were most unwilling to concede. In Soviet correspondents' wartime dispatches, all references to explicitly Jewish suffering were excised by the censor. In 1945, when Russians heaped abuse on their defeated enemies, thoughtful Germans noticed that almost the only charge not laid at their door was that of persecuting the Jews.

In Poland, where anti-semitism was widespread, some people cited reports that Jews had welcomed the Red Army in September 1939 as evidence of their perfidy. In the spring of 1944 some Jewish soldiers deserted from the Polish corps based in Scotland, citing disgust about anti-semitism, which they said was no less apparent in the exile army than in their homeland. Anglo-Saxons were not immune from such sentiments. Even in June 1945, when the concentration camps had been exposed to the world, an increasingly deranged General George Patton denounced liberals who 'believe that the displaced person is a human being, which he is not, and this applied particularly to the Jews, who are lower than animals'.

Though Churchill denounced in the most passionate terms reports of the Nazi extermination programme, his government – like that of Franklin Roosevelt – was unwilling to accept large numbers of Jewish refugees, even if the Germans could be persuaded to release or trade them. When Americans were polled in November 1938 about whether they believed Jewish fugitives from Hitler should be granted special immigration rights to enter the US, 23% said yes, 77% no. A British Colonial Office official commented cynically on a December 1942 report about the death camps: 'Familiar stuff. The Jews have spoilt their case by laying it on too thick for years past.' British intelligence officer Noel Annan wrote of his own state of knowledge about the fate of Europe's Jews in 1944:

It took some time… for the enormity of Germany's crimes against the Jews to sink in. In intelligence we knew of the gas ovens, but not of the scale, the thoroughness, the bureaucratic efficiency with which Jews had been hunted down and slaughtered. No one at the end of the war, as I recollect, realised that the figure of Jewish dead ran into millions.

American diplomat George Ball wrote later:

Perhaps we were so preoccupied with the squalid menace of the war we did not focus on this unspeakable ghastliness. It may also be that the idea of mass extermination was so far beyond the traditional comprehension of most Americans that we instinctively refused to believe in its existence.

It was to the perverse credit of British and American decency that many people were reluctant to suppose their enemies as barbaric as later evidence showed them to have been. None of this diminishes in the smallest degree the responsibility of the Nazis, and of the German people, for the Holocaust. But it should be acknowledged that, even when overwhelming evidence became available, the Allied nations were slow to respond to the death camps. Even if Jews were not persecuted in the Anglo-Saxon societies, nor were they widely loved. There remained until 1945 a resolute official unwillingness to assess their tragedy in a separate dimension from the sufferings of Hitler's other captives, and of the occupied societies of Europe. Such insensitivity merits understanding, but rightly troubles posterity.

Responsibility for executing the genocide programme was entrusted to the SS's deputy chief, Reinhard Heydrich, to whom Himmler later paid a fulsome posthumous tribute:

He was a character of rare purity with an intelligence of penetrating greatness and clarity. He was filled with an incorruptible sense of justice. Truthful and decent people could always rely on his chivalrous sentiment and humane understanding.

These virtues were skilfully concealed on 20 January 1942, when at the Wannsee conference Heydrich mapped the road to the death camps. The intended outcome was no longer in doubt: the 'Final Solution' of the Jewish problem would be accomplished in stages, only the last of which must await the war's end.

There was considerable detailed discussion about the construction of extermination camps and the virtues of gas. The principal outcome of the conference was agreement that the SS would in future exercise absolute authority over the fate of Europe's Jews, and that henceforward, policy would be directed towards the overarching aim of cleansing the entire Nazi empire. This was implemented with remarkable speed: in mid-March 1942, almost three-quarters of all those who perished in the Holocaust were still alive; eleven months later, the same proportion was dead.

Posterity is fascinated by the ease with which the Nazis found so many ordinary men – to borrow the title of Christopher Browning's classic study – willing to murder in cold blood vast numbers of innocents, of all ages and both sexes. Yet there is ample evidence in modern experience that many people are ready to kill others to order, once satisfied that this fulfils the wishes of those whose authority they accept. Hundreds of thousands of Russians were complicit in the deaths of millions of their fellow-countrymen at the behest of Stalin and Beria, before the Holocaust was thought of. Germany's generals may not themselves have killed civilians, but they were happy to acquiesce in others doing so.

Post-war testimony shows that implementation of the Final Solution required only a modicum of patience and practice, to overcome the scruples of some novice mass-murderers. On 13 July 1942, Reserve Police Battalion 101 arrived in a convoy of trucks at the Polish village of Josefow, whose inhabitants included 1,800 Jews. Mostly middle-aged reservists from Hamburg, on their arrival they were ordered to gather around their commander, 53-year-old Major Wilhelm Trapp, a career policeman affectionately known to the unit as 'Papa Trapp'. In a choking voice and with tears in his eyes, he told them they had a most unwelcome assignment, ordered at the highest level: to arrest all Jews in the village, remove to a work camp men of working age, and kill the remainder. He said this was justified by Jewish involvement with partisans, and the Jews' instigation of the American boycott that had injured Germany. He then invited any man who felt unable to perform this unpleasant duty to step aside. Several policemen indeed declined to participate, and after the killings began their number increased. At least 20 were permitted to return to barracks.

Yet a sufficiency of others stayed to do the business: one man later recalled that his first victim vainly begged for mercy, on the grounds that he was a decorated World War One veteran. Georg Kageler, a 37-year-old tailor, killed his first batch easily enough, but then fell into conversation with a mother and daughter from Kassel, who were destined to die next. He appealed to his platoon leader to be excused, and was sent to guard the marketplace while others did his share of shooting.

Christopher Browning shows that during the weeks and months that followed, most of Reserve Police Battalion 101's members overcame initial revulsion, and became hardened killers. Browning found no evidence that any sanction was imposed upon those who refused to kill; in one of the most highly educated societies in Europe, it was easy to find men willing to murder those whom their rulers defined as state enemies, without employing duress.

While a vast number of Germans were directly or indirectly complicit in the massacre of the Jews, a small minority displayed high courage in succouring the persecuted, at mortal risk to themselves. A Jewish fugitive named Max Krakauer compiled a list at the end of the war of all those Berliners who had assisted his long struggle to escape death, and recalled 66 names. Such extraordinarily courageous people sustained a shred of the honour of German civilisation.

KILLING IN POLAND
A member of the SS prepares to shoot a Polish Jew

EUROPE BECOMES A BATTLEFIELD

O n 3 November 1943, Hitler announced to his generals a strategic decision that no further reinforcements would be dispatched to the Eastern Front. He reasoned that German forces still held a wide buffer zone protecting the Reich from the Russians; he must reinforce Italy, where Anglo-American armies were established, and France, where they were certain soon to land.

Yet even as he sought to address the western threats the Russians renewed their assaults in the north. Strategic retreat was the obvious response, because the German threat to Leningrad was no longer credible; but the Führer, after some vacillation, once more insisted that his forces should hold their positions. 'Hitler could think only in lines, not in movements,' sighed a German officer, Rolf-Helmut Schroder, long afterwards. 'If he had allowed his generals to do their job, so much could have been different.'

In May 1944, 2.2 million German troops confronted the Russians; Hitler derived comfort from the fact that the enemy was still 560 miles from Berlin. He believed the main Soviet summer effort would come in north Ukraine, and apportioned his strength accordingly. But he was wrong: the objectives of Zhukov's impending Operation *Bagration*, most spectacular Soviet offensive of the war, lay in the zone defended by Army Group Centre.

Just praise has been lavished upon the ingenuity and success of British and

American deception operations in World War II, but less attention has been paid to the matching achievement of Soviet *maskirovka*, literally 'camouflage'. This attained its zenith in deluding the enemy about the objectives of *Bagration*. Large resources were committed to building dummy tanks, guns and installations, to persuade the Germans that the main Russian thrust would come in north Ukraine, where fake roads and crossings were also created. The Wehrmacht's eastern intelligence chief, the highly regarded Reinhard Gehlen, was entirely misled by the Russian *maskirovka*, as skilful and significant as Anglo-American deceptions before D-Day. The collapse of Hitler's residual illusions in the east waited only upon Russian readiness to strike.

Around the world, cynicism persisted about the modest Anglo-American contribution to the struggle, compared with that of the Soviets. Successive Allied attacks on German positions around Monte Cassino in Italy were characterised by lack of co-ordination, imagination, and indeed competence. The sixth-century Benedictine monastery was battered into rubble; thousands of tons of bombs and shells were expended; many British, Indian, New Zealand and Polish lives were lost; but still the Germans held on.

The Anglo-American corps which landed on the coast further north at Anzio in January, in fulfilment of Churchill's personal vision, was confined to a narrow perimeter which the Germans attacked fiercely and repeatedly. 'So back we go to World War I,' wrote a young officer of a Scottish regiment holding the line there. 'I never saw so many people killed around me before in all my life,' said an Irish Guards corporal. An NCO, watching appalled as swine snuffled around the bodies of the dead in No Man's Land, mused bitterly: 'Is this what we are fighting for, to be eaten by pigs?'

Meanwhile, further south, the Allies were still pinned in the mountains. Once it became clear that decisive victory in the Italian theatre remained unattainable, to Churchill's fury the Americans insisted upon winding down the campaign: they withdrew six US and French divisions to join the battle for France.

In the late spring of 1944 Hitler knew that, within weeks, his armies must face a major Russian offensive. It was vital first to repulse the Anglo-American invasion of France, which was plainly imminent. On the Allied side, there was a matching awareness of the stakes. Amphibious operations in the Mediterranean had done nothing to promote complacency: in Sicily, and again at Salerno and Anzio, forces had landed in chaos, and come within a hair's breadth of disaster. The British had always been apprehensive about fighting a big battle in France, and only relentless American pressure on Britain's leadership enforced the D-Day commitment.

NORMANDY, JUNE 1944
*Soldiers disembark on the
French coast*

Churchill and Roosevelt, however, deserved their nations' gratitude for delaying D-Day until 1944, when their own resources had become so large, and those of Hitler were so shrunken; Allied losses in the ensuing continental campaign were a fraction of what they must have been had D-Day taken place earlier. For the young men who made the assault on 6 June 1944, however, such grand truths meant nothing: they recognised only the mortal peril each one must face, to breach Hitler's Atlantic Wall.

The invasion began with drops by one British and two American airborne divisions on the night of 5 June. The airborne landings were chaotic but achieved their objectives, confusing the Germans and securing the flanks of the assault zone; paratroopers engaged enemy forces wherever they encountered them with an energy worthy of such elite formations.

Sgt. Mickey McCallum never forgot his first firefight, a few hours after landing: a German machine-gunner mortally wounded the man next to him, Private Bill Attlee. McCallum asked Attlee 'if he was hit bad'. The soldier replied: 'I'm dying Sergeant Mickey, but we are going to win this damn war, aren't we? You damn well A we are.' In the hours and days that followed, many other such young men displayed similar spirit and were obliged to make a matching sacrifice. At dawn on 6 June, six infantry divisions with supporting armour struck the beaches of Normandy across a 30-mile front; one Canadian and two British formations landed on the left, three American divisions on the right.

Operation *Overlord* was the greatest combined operation in history. Some 5,300 ships carried 150,000 men and 1,500 tanks, scheduled to land in the first wave, supported by 12,000 aircraft. On the French coast that morning, a drama unfolded in three dimensions such as the world would never behold again. British and Canadian troops poured ashore at *Sword*, *Juno* and *Gold* beaches, exploiting innovative armoured technology to overwhelm the defences, many of them manned by *ostruppen* of Hitler's empire.

The Americans seized *Utah*, the elbow of the Cherbourg peninsula, with only small loss. 'You know, it sounds kind of dumb, but it was just like an exercise,' said a private soldier wonderingly. 'We waded ashore like kids in a crocodile and up the beach. A couple of shells came over but nowhere near us. I think I even felt somehow disappointed, a little let down.' Further east at *Omaha* beach, however, Americans suffered the heaviest casualties of the day – more than 800 killed.

When news of the invasion was broadcast, across the Allied nations churches filled with unaccustomed worshippers, joining prayers for the men of the armies. Industrial strikes were abandoned and civilian blood donations soared. In Europe, millions of oppressed and threatened people experienced a thrill of emotion.

On the beaches, reinforcements poured ashore from shuttling landing craft, so that by the end of D+1 (the day after D-Day) Montgomery deployed 450,000 men. The first Allied fighters began to fly from improvised local airstrips; the Luftwaffe was so shrunken by months of attrition over Germany that its planes scarcely troubled the invaders. The D-Day battle cost only 3,000 British, American and Canadian dead, a negligible price for a decisive strategic achievement. The people of Normandy, however, suffered terribly for their liberation, losing as many dead on 6 June as the invaders. Allied bombs and shells killed some 20,000 people in north-west France during the bitter attritional fighting that now began.

Eisenhower and his generals had always recognised that the 'battle of the build-up' in the weeks following D-Day would be as critical as the landings: if the Germans could concentrate forces in Normandy more swiftly than the Allies, the invaders might still be evicted. Deception planners made a vital contribution, by their brilliantly sophisticated Operation *Fortitude*, which convinced the Germans of a continuing threat to the Pas De Calais, where important forces lingered for weeks. But the 11-week campaign which followed became by far the most costly of the Western war, and Normandy the only battlefield where casualty rates briefly matched those of the Eastern front.

Though D-Day had huge symbolic significance and commands the fascination of posterity, the fighting that followed was much bloodier: for instance, while D Company of the British Ox & Bucks regiment triumphantly seized 'Pegasus bridge' across the Caen canal early on 6 June for the loss of only two killed and 14 wounded, next day it suffered 60 casualties in an inconclusive little action at Escoville. Brigadier Frank Richardson, one of Montgomery's ablest staff officers, wrote afterwards of the Germans, whom he admired boundlessly: 'I have often wondered how we ever beat them.'

But the Allies' most serious problem was the inferiority of their tanks: numerical advantage counted for little, when British and American shells often bounced off well-armoured German Panthers and Tigers, while a hit on a Sherman, Churchill or Cromwell was almost invariably fatal.

Meanwhile, in Berlin, Hitler confronted an even graver threat: less than three weeks after the landings in France, in the east the Soviets launched Operation *Bagration*, which became the greatest offensive of the war.

The Red Army advanced more swiftly than Eisenhower's forces in 1944-45, partly because its soldiers lived off the land and required much lower scales of supply: they were the least cosseted of the war. Poles had a dark joke in

1944, about a bird which falls out of the sky into a cowpat, to be rescued by a cat; its moral, they claimed, was that 'not everyone who gets you out of the shit is necessarily your friend'. The Soviet 'liberation' of Poland, which began with *Bagration*, obliged its people to exchange the rule of one tyranny for another. The Russians murdered thousands of Poles whose only crime was a commitment to democratic freedom; most notoriously, they declined to succour the August Warsaw Uprising. Russians nursed a historic hatred for the Polish people, and indulged this in 1944-45 with indiscriminate savagery towards both sexes.

Hitler's generals knew that the Wehrmacht could only delay the inevitable; if great wars were ever fought rationally, the moment had come for Germany to surrender. But he had committed himself to a policy of total, indeed perpetual, war; if he was to be denied victory, in the last months of his rule he seemed content instead to preside over a titanic final cataclysm, matching in scale the failure of his titanic ambitions.

Posterity is more puzzled by the failure of other Germans to accept the logic of their predicament, to depose the Nazis and save hundreds of thousands of lives by abandoning the struggle. Such an initiative could only credibly have come from the generals. The 20 July 1944 bomb plot, the only concerted military attempt to decapitate the Nazi regime, was conducted with stunning incompetence and lack of conviction, and engaged a relatively small number of officers. A legend of anti-Nazi resistance was created, and is today sustained, chiefly to bolster the revival of post-war German self-esteem. Colonel Claus von Stauffenburg would almost certainly have been successful in killing Hitler had he remained in the Führer's headquarters to detonate his bomb instead of hastening back to Berlin. Many other officers had opportunities to achieve the same end, at the sacrifice of their own lives.

As it was, a perverted sense of duty caused most of the Wehrmacht's leadership to follow the Nazi regime to the end, to their perpetual dishonour. Among themselves, Germany's generals often mocked the character and conduct of the gangsters and grotesques by whom their country was led; yet their slavishness towards Hitler seldom flagged. At a meeting on 27 January 1944, when he called on every officer to display loyal and fanatical support for National Socialism, Manstein called out: 'And so it will be, My Führer!' Manstein later claimed that his interjection was intended ironically, but few believed him.

The soldiers abandoned the civilians to their despair. In Hamburg, old Mathilde Wolfe-Monckeburg wrote on 25 June 1944: 'No one ever laughs any more, no one is light-hearted or happy... We are waiting for the final act.'

LIBERATION
Italian soldiers greet loved ones after Rome falls to the Allies

Germany's military leaders earned the contempt of posterity for indulging the mass-murderers who led their country, while claiming to absolve themselves of complicity in the Nazis' crimes; to contemplate revolt in the last phase of a struggle for national survival demanded a moral courage such as few German officers displayed. They knew the carnage they had wreaked in Russia: they could expect no mercy from Stalin's people, and fear of impending Soviet vengeance became a dominant motivation for millions of German soldiers. It provided a perverse and spurious justification for the generals' refusal to contemplate turning on Hitler. Their reasoning was vacuous, because sustained resistance merely delayed the inevitable; yet even the more intelligent clung to fantastic hopes that the Western Allies would deliver them from the Russians

The Wehrmacht's performance can partly be explained by compulsion – the fact that deserters and alleged cowards were ruthlessly shot, in their thousands during the last months. Between 1914 and 1918, 150 death sentences were passed on members of the Kaiser's army, of which just 48 were carried out. By contrast, between 1939 and 1945 more than 15,000 military executions were officially listed, and the real total was substantially higher.

As the Allies advanced across northern France, the Germans abandoned Paris without a fight. General Jacques Leclerc's Free French armoured division entered the capital on 25 August 1944 to find the Resistance claiming possession, a legend that began the resurrection of France's national self-respect. The Allied armies embarked on a dramatic pursuit which carried them into eastern Belgium and the liberation of Brussels. On 1 September, Eisenhower assumed operational command of the Anglo-American forces, relegating Montgomery, who had been directing US and British ground forces, to leadership of the Anglo-Canadian 21st Army Group with the sop of promotion to field marshal. The Western Allies were convinced that by achieving victory in Normandy they had brought Germany to the verge of defeat. Most of France was free, at a cost of only 40,000 dead.

CHAPTER SIXTEEN

GERMANY BESIEGED

In the first days of September 1944, much of the Allied leadership – with the notable exception of Winston Churchill – supposed their nations within weeks of completing the conquest of the Third Reich. Many Germans were of the same opinion, making grim preparations for the moment when invaders would sweep their country.

The German people understood that if the Russians broke through in the east, all was lost. 'Then there'll be nothing left but to take poison,' a Hamburg neighbour told Mathilde Wolfe-Monckeburg 'quite calmly, as if she was suggesting pancakes for dinner tomorrow'.

Most of Germany's cities were already devastated by bombing. Emmy Suppanz wrote to her son on the Western front from Marburg, describing life at home:

> Café Kaefer is still open from 6.30 to 9am and from 5 to 10 or 11pm. Bits of plaster moulding fell off the ceilings in the last attack, though oddly enough the mirrors are still unbroken. The windows in the café and the flat above have gone, of course. Burschi had two rabbits, one fairly big white one called Hansi and a smaller grey one to which we had not yet given a name, and was eaten a fortnight ago.

Such news from home ate deep into the spirit of soldiers far away, fighting for their lives.

PREPARING FOR INVASION
Eisenhower talks to paratroopers before D Day

With the Germans on their knees, unprecedented rewards seemed available for risk-taking: Montgomery persuaded Eisenhower that in his own northern sector of the front, there was an opportunity to launch a war-winning thrust, to seize a bridge over the Rhine at the Dutch town of Arnhem, across which Allied forces might flood into Germany.

It remains a focus of fierce controversy whether the Western Allied armies should have been able to win the war in 1944, following the Wehrmacht's collapse in France. But the Allies still lacked a usable major port. The French rail system was largely wrecked. The movement of fuel, ammunition and supplies for two million men by roads alone posed enormous problems: almost every ton of supplies had to be trucked hundreds of miles from the beaches to the armies. 'Until we get Antwerp,' Eisenhower wrote to General George Marshall, 'we are always going to be operating on a shoestring.' In much the same fashion that the Wehrmacht allowed the British to escape from the continent amid German euphoria in 1940, an outbreak of Allied 'victory disease' permitted their enemies now to regroup. By the time Montgomery launched his ambitious dash for a bridge across the Rhine, the Germans had regained their balance.

On 17 September, three Allied airborne divisions landed in Holland: the US 82nd and 101st were tasked to seize river and canal crossings between the Allied front line and Arnhem; the British 1st Airborne to capture the Rhine bridge and hold a perimeter beyond it. The American operations were largely successful. The British, however, ran into immediate difficulties. The decision to drop 1st Airborne outside Arnhem imposed a four-hour pause between the opening of the first parachute canopies and Lt. Col. John Frost's arrival on foot at the bridge; this provided the Germans in their vehicles with far too generous a margin of time to respond.

There was an even more fundamental flaw in Montgomery's plan, which would probably have scotched his ambitions even if British paratroopers had secured both sides of the bridge: the relieving force needed to cover the 59 miles from the Meuse-Escaut Canal to Arnhem in three days, with access to only a single Dutch road.

The Allied advance was soon behind schedule. The Germans were able to make their own deployments in full knowledge of Allied intentions, because they found the operational plan for *Market Garden* on the body of a US staff officer who had recklessly carried it into battle; within hours, the document was on the desk of General Model, who exploited his insight to the full.

Apologists for *Market Garden*, in which 1,485 British paratroopers were killed, asserted that it achieved substantial success, by leaving the Allies in possession of a deep salient into Holland. This was nonsense. The Arnhem assault was a flawed concept for which the chances of success were negligible. The British commanders charged with executing it, notably Lt. Gen. Frederick 'Boy' Browning, displayed shameful incompetence, and merited dismissal with ignominy rather than the honours they received, in a classic British propaganda operation intended to dignify disaster. Montgomery's ambition personally to deliver a war-winning thrust, fortified by conceit, caused him to undertake the only big operation for which the Allied armies could generate logistic support that autumn, across the terrain least suited to its success.

The western Allies lost a small chance of breaking into Germany in September – small, because probability suggests that they lacked sufficient combat power to win the war in 1944. They lacked the energy and imagination to improvise expedients to overcome their supply problems, as an advancing German army might have done. And from October onwards, the weather reinforced the Germans, imposing stagnation across the front.

The winter of 1944 proved one of the wettest for decades in western Europe. It is hard for civilians to comprehend the miseries of an outdoor existence week after week and month after month in such conditions. 'With our tent and clothing wet and half-frozen,' wrote American soldier George Neill, 'I felt numb to the point of almost not caring what happened to me.' Airborne soldier Pfc Bill True was intensely moved when, one evening, a little girl approached the foxhole occupied by himself and another man, and handed them two pillows. Here was a tiny, innocent gesture towards decencies of civilisation which otherwise seemed immeasurably remote.

Against the impassioned opposition of his generals, Hitler now launched a Western offensive, at the place the Allied least expected it – the Ardennes forest, on the frontiers of Germany, Belgium and Luxemburg. The objective was to reach Antwerp, splitting the Allied front; to execute it, two new panzer armies were created, 30 divisions assembled, reserves of precious fuel stockpiled.

On 18 December, Operation *Autumn Mist* was launched against the weakest sector of General Hodges's First US Army. It achieved absolute tactical and strategic surprise, a breakthrough on a 40-mile wide front as panic-stricken American troops broke and fled in disarray in the path of the SS panzers; amid thick fog, the Allied air forces were impotent to intervene. Within two days, German troops were pouring through a gaping hole – 'the bulge' – in the American line.

Lt. Tony Moody was one of a host of young Americans who found themselves overwhelmed by the experience of retreat: 'We were so tired, out of rations, low on ammo. There was panic, there was chaos.' 'Fear reigned,' wrote Donald Burgett. His formation, the 101st Airborne, played a critical part in stabilising the front, while watching soldiers of some other units flee for their lives. 'Once fear strikes, it spreads like an epidemic, faster than wildfire. Once the first man runs, others soon follow. Then, it's all over; soon there are hordes of men running, all of them wild-eyed and driven by fear.'

The Germans, during their brief reoccupation of liberated Belgian towns and villages, found time to execute scores of civilians either deemed guilty of resistance activity, or murdered merely as examples to others. The savagery of some of Model's men reflected a venom characteristic of 1944-45: if they themselves were doomed to lose the war and probably to die, they were bent upon depriving as many enemies as possible of the joys of survival and liberation.

But the Germans were desperately short of tanks, aircraft, fuel and quality manpower and by 3 January Hodges's and Patton's armies were counter-attacking north and south, while Model's remaining tanks had exhausted their fuel and momentum. Wehrmacht infantry captain Rolf-Helmut Schröder said of his own part in the Bulge: 'We finished the battle where we had started it; then I knew – that's it.' Germany losing the war, he acknowledged, was now inevitable.

The Allies lacked sufficient nerve to attempt to cut off the German retreat. Eisenhower was content merely to restore his front, after suffering the most traumatic shock of the north-west Europe campaign. The Ardennes battle left a legacy of caution which persisted until the end of the war. 'Americans are not brought up on disaster as are the British, to whom this was merely one more incident on the inevitably rough road towards final victory,' in the sardonic words of Sir Frederick Morgan. 'The record of accomplishment is essentially bland and plodding,' wrote the magisterial American historian Martin Blumenson. 'The commanders were generally workmanlike rather than bold, prudent rather than daring, George S. Patton being of course a notable exception.'

The worst victims of the Ardennes offensive were the German people. Most now cherished ambitions only to see the Western Allies, rather than the Russians, occupy their cities and villages. The Russians, meanwhile, became important beneficiaries of Hitler's losses: when they launched their own great offensive on 12 January, many of the German tanks which might have checked their advance lay wrecked on the Western Front. The Ardennes battle, by dissipating Hitler's armoured reserves, hastened Germany's end. It also ensured that the Red Army, rather than the Americans and British, led the way to Hitler's capital.

CHAPTER SEVENTEEN

THE FALL OF THE THIRD REICH

At the end of October 1944, Heinrich Himmler delivered an apocalyptic speech in East Prussia, setting the stage for the final defence of the Reich:

> Our enemies must know that every kilometre they seek to advance into our country will cost them rivers of blood. They will step onto a field of human mines consisting of fanatical uncompromising fighters; every block of city flats, village, farmstead, forest will be defended by men, boys and old men and, if need be, by women and girls.

On the Eastern Front during the months that followed, his vision was largely fulfilled: 1.2 million German troops and around a quarter of million civilians died during the futile struggle to check the Russian onslaught; so, too, did many people whose governments had rashly allied themselves with the Third Reich in its years of European dominance, or who volunteered to serve the Nazi cause.

Among those who found themselves in the path of the Soviet juggernaut were the nine million people of Hungary, who found an ironic black humour in reminding each other that their nation had been defeated in every war in which it had participated for 500 years. Now, they faced the consequences of espousing the losing side in the most terrible conflict of all. Early in December 1944, the Russians forced a passage of the Danube under withering fire, with their usual indifference to casualties.

On 30 December, a thousand Russian guns opened a barrage on Budapest which continued for ten hours daily, with air raids in between. Civilians huddled in their cellars, which failed to protect many from incineration or asphyxiation. In some places the Russians drove prisoners in front of them, who shouted despairingly, 'We are Hungarians!' before both sides' fire tore into them.

Hunger gnawed every man, woman and child. The Budapest garrison's 25,000 horses were eaten. Only 14 of 2,500 animals in the city's zoo survived – the rest were killed by Soviet fire or slaughtered for meat; for weeks, a lion roamed the underground rail tunnels, until captured by a Soviet task force dispatched for the purpose. Starving civilians were shot out of hand for raiding parachuted containers in search of food. In the maternity ward of a hospital, nurses clutched motherless babies to their breasts to provide at least human warmth, as the starving infants drifted towards death. Throughout the siege, the persecution and murder of Budapest's Jews continued.

The capture of Budapest cost the Russians around 80,000 dead and a quarter of a million wounded. Some 38,000 civilians died in the siege; tens of thousands more were deported to the Soviet Union for forced labour, from which many never returned. The German and Hungarian forces lost about 40,000 dead. This savage, futile battle would have been accounted an epic had it taken place on the Anglo-American front. As it was, only the Hungarians took much notice of its horrors then or later. Within three months, it was eclipsed by a matching drama, on a much larger scale, in Hitler's own capital.

The bulk of the Wehrmacht and Waffen SS now faced the armies of Zhukov, Konev and Rokossovsky; the Russians deployed 6.7 million men on a front extending from the Baltic to the Adriatic. The final death grapple between the forces of the two rival tyrants, Stalin and Hitler, was among the most terrible military encounters of the war, while Eisenhower's armies occupied the edge of the stage.

The Allied occupation zones had been agreed many months earlier, and confirmed at the February Yalta summit. To spare central Europe from a Soviet tyranny in succession to that of the Nazis, it would have been necessary for the Allies to fight a very different and more ruthless war, at much higher cost in casualties. They would have had to acknowledge the possibility, even probability, of fighting the Red Army as well as the Wehrmacht. Such a course was politically and militarily unthinkable, whatever Churchill's brief delusions

YALTA 1945
Churchill, Roosevelt and Stalin

that East European freedom could be secured by force.

There was a further consideration: the Russians were desperate to secure the Nazis' nuclear scientists and research material. Knowing from his agents in the West that the Americans were close to perfecting an atomic bomb, Stalin wanted everything that would help to kick-start the rival Soviet project: the Kaiser Wilhelm Institute for Physics in Dahlem was identified as a vital objective for the Red Army.

On 12 January 1945, the Soviets launched a general offensive out of their Vistula bridgeheads: outnumbering the defenders by ten to one, their tanks and infantry streamed westward, crushing everything in their path. During the last four months of the war, more Germans perished than in the whole of 1942-43. Such numbers emphasise the price paid by the German people for their army leadership's failure to depose the Nazis and quit the war before its last terrible act. Landowners in East Prussia and Pomerania rash enough to remain in their homes, sometimes because of age or infirmity, suffered terrible fates: to be identified by the invaders not merely as Germans, but also as aristocrats, invited torture before death.

Danish correspondent Jacob Kronika wrote that many Berliners now fervently desired their leader's end. 'Years ago they shouted "Heil!" Now they hate the man who calls himself their Führer.' Behind the front, the Nazis indulged a final orgy of killing: jails were emptied, their occupants shot; almost all surviving opponents of the regime held in concentration camps were executed, and lesser victims massacred with a dreadful carelessness.

A last climactic battle remained. Now, Hitler's capital became the focus of a vast concentration of military power: the three Soviet *fronts* that massed before Berlin comprised 2.5 million men and 6,250 armoured vehicles, supported by 7,500 aircraft. In darkness in the early hours of 16 April, Zhukov launched a frontal assault against the Seelow Heights east of the city. The operation was among the most brutish and unimaginative of Russia's war. Its commander was so impressed by watching his bombardment devastating the defences that after 30 minutes he gave the order to start the attack. A Russian engineer wrote home that night:

Along the whole length of the horizon it was bright as daylight. On the German side, everything was covered with smoke and thick fountains of earth in clumps flying up. There were huge flocks of scared birds flying around in the sky, a constant humming, thunder, explosions. We had to cover our ears to prevent our eardrums breaking. Then tanks began roaring, searchlights were lit along all of the front line in order to blind the Germans. Then people started shouting everywhere, '*Na Berlin!*'

In the battle which followed, General Gotthard Heinrici's defenders inflicted three Soviet casualties for each of their own. There was no display of inspired Soviet generalship: Zhukov's hordes merely threw themselves forward again and again. The Germans poured fire into the attackers, destroying tanks in hundreds, killing men in thousands.

The capture of the Seelow Heights cost the Russians 30,000 dead, the Germans 12,000. The attackers hastened on towards the city along the main road, Reichsstrasse 1, as fugitives and deserters scurried and stumbled to stay ahead of them. 'They all seem so miserable, so little like men any more,' wrote a Berlin woman watching German soldiers shuffle past her apartment building on 22 April. Dorothea von Schwanenflugel described an encounter with one unhappy boy:

a mere child in a uniform many sizes too large for him, with an anti-tank grenade lying beside him. Tears were running down his face, and he was obviously very frightened of everyone. I very softly asked him what he was doing there. He lost his distrust and told me that he had been ordered to lie in wait here, and when a Soviet tank approached he was to run under it and explode the grenade. I asked how that would work, but he didn't know. In fact this frail child didn't even look capable of carrying such a grenade.

With so many Germans running away or surrendering, it is extraordinary that resistance persisted for so long. Some 45,000 SS and Wehrmacht troops, together with 40,000 Volkssturm and a mere 60 tanks, held out for a week against the might of Zhukov's and Konev's armies. In Hitler's capital, the Red Army paid the price for its policy of unrestrained savagery towards German soldiers and civilians: it is hard to suppose that Berlin's defenders would have fought so stubbornly had they entertained hopes of mercy for themselves or the population. As it was, the Soviet commitment to murder, rape and pillage was known to every German; most of those manning the perimeter saw no prospect save that of death.

Russians and Germans alike were mocked by the contrast between the mountains of wreckage, heaped and broken bodies, littering the landscape, and signs of spring breaking through: when gunfire paused even briefly, birds could be heard singing; trees blossomed until blast reduced them to blackened skeletons; tulips flowered in some places, and amid the parks there was an overpowering scent of lilac. But mostly there were corpses. Germany's leaders had conducted a long love affair with death: in Berlin in April 1945, this achieved a final consummation.

On the afternoon of the 30th, as Russian troops stormed the Reichstag building 400 yards from Hitler's bunker, the leader of the Third Reich killed himself and his wife. The banality of evil has seldom been more vividly displayed than by their conduct in their last days. Eva Braun was much preoccupied with the disposal of her jewellery – 'my diamond watch is unfortunately being repaired' – and by concealing her dressmakers' accounts from posterity: 'On no account must Heise's bills be found.' She wrote in a last letter to her friend Herta Ostermayr: 'What should I say to you? I cannot understand how it should have all come to this, but it is impossible to believe any more in a God.'

Most Germans received the news of Hitler's death with numbed indifference. In the capital sporadic fighting persisted for two more days, until Berlin's commandant Lt. Gen. Karl Wiedling surrendered on 2 May.

Everywhere the Soviet victors held sway, they embarked upon an orgy of celebration, rape and destruction on a scale such as Europe had not witnessed since the 17th Century. 'The baker comes stumbling towards me down the hall,' wrote a Berlin woman about one of her neighbours, 'white as his flour, holding out his hands: "They have my wife..."' A German lawyer, who had miraculously preserved his Jewish wife through the Nazi years, now sought to protect her from Russian soldiers. One shot him in the hip. As he lay dying, he saw three men rape her as she screamed out her own Jewish identity.

Stalin was untroubled by the behaviour of his soldiers towards the Germans – or to their supposedly liberated slaves. The Soviets saw no shame, such as burdens Western societies, about the concept of revenge. The war had been fought chiefly on Russian soil. The Russian people had endured sufferings incomparably greater than those of the Americans and British. As conquerors, the Germans had behaved barbarously, their conduct rendered the more base because they spoke so much of honour, and professed adherence to civilised values. Now the Soviet Union exacted a terrible punishment. The German nation had brought misery on the world, and in 1945 it paid. The price of having started and lost a war against a tyranny as ruthless as Stalin's was that vengeance was exacted on terms almost as merciless as those Hitler's minions had imposed on Europe since 1939.

CHAPTER EIGHTEEN

JAPAN: DEFYING FATE

During 1944, the US Navy gained overwhelming dominance of the Pacific. American submarines achieved the strangulation of Japanese commerce which Germany's U-boats had failed to impose on Britain. Seldom in history has such a small force – some 16,000 men, 1.6% of the sea service's strength, with never more than 50 boats deployed – gained such decisive results. It is extraordinary that Hirohito's nation went to war knowing the importance and vulnerability of its merchant shipping, yet without seriously addressing convoy protection; the Tokyo regime built huge warships for the Combined Fleet, but grossly inadequate numbers of escorts.

Japanese island garrisons found themselves isolated, immobilised and starving.

It was rationally unnecessary for the Allies to launch major ground operations in south-east Asia; if they merely maintained naval blockade and air bombardment, the Japanese people must eventually starve. Given the nature of war, democracies and global geopolitics, however, 'eventually' was not soon enough. In the spring of 1944, it was taken for granted that Allied forces must attack the Japanese wherever possible, and, by then, the United States was producing so many ships and planes that it felt able to commit large forces to the Pacific.

Service in the Pacific was an experience light years from that of Europe, first because of its geographical isolation. US Marine pilot Samuel Hynes wrote: 'Out here the war life was all there was; no history was visible, no monuments

of the past, no cities remembered from books. There was nothing here to remind a soldier of his other life; no towns, no bars, nowhere to go, nowhere even to desert to.' Men obliged to exist for months under open skies in tropical conditions suffered relentlessly from disease and skin disorders, even before enemy action took a bloodier toll.

The most important Pacific operation of 1944 was the seizure of the Marianas, key to the inner ring of Japan's defences. When the US Marine Corps began its assaults on Saipan, Tinian and Guam, the Japanese Combined Fleet sailed to meet the invaders; the outcome was the greatest carrier encounter of the war. Both sides deployed formidable forces, but the Americans outnumbered the Japanese by around two to one at sea and in the air, and what followed became known as 'the great Marianas turkey-shoot': of Admiral Jizaburo Ozawa's 373 planes dispatched, only 130 survived, having failed to inflict significant damage on the US fleet.

But victory at sea off the Marianas could not avert bloody fighting ashore. And in the south-west Pacific the US was conducting a much more controversial campaign. General Douglas MacArthur, the regional supreme commander, was bent upon personally achieving the liberation of the 17 million people of the Philippines, where he had spent much of his own service life.

On 20 October 1944, four army divisions began to land on Leyte island, in the midst of the Philippines. They met light opposition, and by afternoon the beachhead was sufficiently secure for MacArthur to stride ashore himself and deliver a grandiloquent liberation broadcast. Thereafter, however, increasingly vigorous Japanese resistance turned the battle into an ordeal by rain, mud and blood for tens of thousands of US soldiers.

On 9 January 1945 US forces landed on the main Philippine island of Luzon, to begin a campaign which lasted for the rest of the war, against Japanese forces directed with stubborn skill by Gen. Tomoyoki Yamashita, the 1942 'Tiger of Malaya'. Manila, the capital, was razed to the ground during weeks of fighting, in which forces of Japanese sailors fought almost to the last man. These men also committed massacres of civilians which lacked the smallest military purpose, but demonstrated Japan's determination to impose on every victim within reach death, often accompanied by rape and mutilation, before meeting their own fate.

The Filipino people whom MacArthur professed to love paid the price for his egomania in lost lives – something approaching half a million perished by combat, massacre, famine and disease – and wrecked homes. It was as great a misfortune for them as for the Allied war effort that neither President Roosevelt nor the US chiefs of staffs could contain MacArthur's ambitions within a smaller compass of folly. In 1944, America's advance to victory over Japan was inexorable, but the follies of the South-West Pacific Supreme Commander disfigured its achievement.

In the spring of 1945, Indian and British forces led by General Bill Slim conducted a brilliantly successful campaign to recapture Burma. This was irrelevant to the outcome of the war. But it did something to restore the battered confidence and fallen prestige of the British Empire.

Slim's army, dominated by Indian troops, was much stronger than that of the Japanese and supported by powerful armoured and air forces. Its chief problem was to supply an advance across mountainous and densely-vegetated country almost bereft of roads. Air dropping, made possible by a large commitment of US planes, became a critical factor in the campaign. The Japanese army had lost almost all its guns and vehicles. It sustained isolated pockets of resistance to the end of the war, but faced slaughter as shattered units sought to break through Slim's army. In the last months, the British suffered only a few hundred casualties, while the 1945 Burma campaign cost their enemies 80,000 dead.

The main business of closing the ring on Japan was meanwhile being done in the Pacific. In February, three US Marine divisions landed on Iwo Jima, an island pimple 3,000 miles west of Pearl Harbor. But the defenders were well prepared and deeply dug in and by 27 March, when Iwo Jima was finally secured, the Americans had suffered some 24,000 casualties, including 7,184 dead, to capture an island one-third the size of Manhattan. Then, in April, came the American landing on Okinawa, designed to pave the way for what threatened to be the bloodiest battle of the Asian war – invasion of the Japanese mainland. But the south of the island had been transformed into a fortress. Again and again US soldiers and Marines thrust forward – and were repulsed.

With the war in Europe coming to an end and the power of the United States everywhere triumphant, it seemed to Americans at home intolerable that their boys should die in thousands to wrest from fanatics a remote and meaningless piece of real estate: there was intense public anger, directed less against the enemy than towards their own commanders. The men fighting on Okinawa shared the American people's frustration. Japan was bleeding from a thousand cuts; all that was now in doubt was how its rulers might be induced to acknowledge their defeat. They believed, however, that a negotiated peace could be won by imposing on the Americans a heavy blood-price for every gain, and sought to emphasise this by mounting a rising tempo of kamikaze air attacks against the US Navy.

As early as 1939, the USAAF's General Carl 'Tooey' Spaatz had anticipated using America's embryo B-29 Superfortress bomber to attack Japan and in 1945 the bomber offensive, after sporadic air raids in 1944, was dramatically transformed and intensified first, by the establishment of a huge network of bases on the Marianas; second, by large deliveries of aircraft; and finally, by the ascent of Lt. Gen. Curtis LeMay to leadership of XX1st Bomber Command. LeMay was architect of the first great fire-raising raid on Tokyo on 9 March 1945. In the 14 months of the USAAF bombing campaign against Japan, 170,000 tons of bombs were dropped, most of these in the last six months; 65 Japanese cities were reduced to ashes. But LeMay's role in punishing Japan for launching a war of aggression was more significant than his contribution to enforcing its surrender.

Stalin had promised to join the eastern war and launch a great Manchurian offensive in August. Against Japan as against Germany, there seemed every prospect that American lives could be saved by allowing the Russians to do some of the bloodiest business of smashing the enemy. Washington was remarkably naïve in failing to recognise that Stalin intended to engage the Japanese not to oblige the United States, but because he was determined to secure his own territorial prizes. Far from requiring inducements to commit his soldiers, the Soviet warlord could not have been deflected from doing so. Of all the belligerents, he sustained the most clear-sighted vision of his own purposes. Through June and July 1945, thousands of Soviet troop trains shuttled eastwards across Asia, carrying armies which had defeated Germany to complete the destruction of Japan.

Meanwhile, at a score of massive, closely-wired installations across the United States, 125,000 scientists, engineers and support staff laboured to bring to fruition the Manhattan Project, greatest and most terrible scientific enterprise of the war.

In 1942, the British had made significant progress with research on an atomic bomb; their theoretical knowledge, indeed, was then greater than that of America's scientists. But, with their own island embattled, they recognised that they lacked resources to build a weapon quickly. An agreement was reached whereby British and European emigre scientists crossed the Atlantic to work with the Americans. Thereafter, Britain's contribution was quickly forgotten in Washington: the United States became brutally proprietorial about its ownership of The Bomb.

Only a small number of scientists grasped the earthshaking significance of atomic power. Maj. Gen. Leslie Groves, directing the Manhattan Project, was wholly untroubled by the agonising of such scientists as Edward Teller who wrote almost despairingly to a colleague: 'I have no hope of clearing my conscience. The things we are working on are so terrible that no amount of protesting or fiddling with politics will save our souls.'

Even Teller, in the end, convinced himself, by no means foolishly, that the best hope for the future of mankind lay in actually using the bomb – a live demonstration which would show the world the insanity of the future use of such weapons in wars. The vast enterprise had a momentum of its own, which only two developments might have checked. First, Truman could have shown extraordinary enlightenment, and decreed that the weapon was too terrible to be employed; more plausibly, the Japanese might have offered their unconditional surrender.

Some of those who are today most critical of the use of the bombs ignore the fact that every day the war continued, prisoners and slaves of the Japanese empire in Asia continued to die in thousands. Truman's greatest mistake, in protecting his own reputation, was failure to deliver an explicit ultimatum before attacking Hiroshima and Nagasaki. The Western Allies' Potsdam Declaration, issued on 26 July, threatened Japan with 'prompt and utter destruction' if it failed to surrender forthwith. This phrase was pregnant with significance for the Allied leaders, who knew that the first atomic bomb had just been successfully tested at Alamagordo. But to the Japanese, it merely heralded more of the same: fire-bombing and eventual invasion.

By the high summer of 1945, Japan's rulers wished to end the war; but its generals were still bent upon securing 'honourable' terms, which included retention of substantial parts of Japan's empire in Manchuria, Korea and China, together with Allied agreement to spare the country from occupation or war crimes indictments. 'No one person in Japan had authority remotely resembling that of an American president,' observes Professor Akira Namamura of Dokkyo university, a modern Japanese historian. 'The Emperor was obliged to act in accordance with the Japanese constitution, which meant that he was obliged to heed the wishes of the Army, Navy and civilian politicians.'

No sane person would suggest that the use of the atomic bombs represented an absolute good, or was even a righteous act. But, in the course of the war, it had been necessary to do many terrible things to advance the cause of Allied victory. By August 1945, to Allied leaders the lives of their own people had come to seem very dear, those of their enemies very cheap. Just as Hitler was the architect of Germany's devastation, the Tokyo regime bore overwhelming responsibility for what took place at Hiroshima and Nagasaki. If Japan's leaders had bowed to logic, as well as to the welfare of their own people, by quitting the war, the atomic bombs would not have been dropped.

When 19-year-old Superfortress gunner Joseph Majeski saw the B-29 *Enola Gay* arrive on Tinian, specially modified to carry only tail armament, he strolled over and asked one of its crew what they had come for. The man answered flippantly 'we're here to win the war', and of course the young airman did not believe him. A few days later, on 6 August 1945, the plane dropped 'Little Boy' on Hiroshima. Its detonation generated the power of 12,500 tons of conventional explosive, created injuries of a kind never before experienced by humankind, and killed at least 70,000 people. Around the world, many people at first found the notion of what had taken place beyond the compass of their imaginations.

Three days later 'Fat Man' was dropped on Nagasaki, matching the explosive power of 22,000 tons of TNT, and killing at least 30,000 people. In the early hours of that day, the first of 1.5 million Soviet troops crossed the border into Manchuria. They swept across the region, overwhelming the hopelessly outgunned Japanese. The brief campaign cost them 12,000 dead, more than the British Army lost in France in 1940, while something close to 80,000 Japanese soldiers perished.

The Emperor Hirohito summoned a gathering of his country's military and political Japanese, and informed them of his determination to end the war. Some senior figures, including the war minister and some generals and admirals, committed ritual suicide, an example followed by several hundred humbler folk. At 1900 on the evening of 14 August Washington time – already the 15th in Japan – Harry Truman read the announcement of Japan's unconditional surrender to a dense throng of politicians and journalists at the White House. In Tokyo Bay on 1 September, Japanese and Allied representatives headed by General Douglas MacArthur signed the surrender document on the deck of the battleship *Missouri*. The Second World War was officially ended.

CHAPTER NINETEEN

VICTORS AND VANQUISHED

Goethe wrote in the early 19th century: 'Our modern wars make many unhappy while they last and none happy when they are over.' So it almost was in 1945. The war ended abruptly in Europe: sullenly or thankfully, millions of Germans surrendered, tossing away their weapons before joining vast columns of prisoners shuffling towards improvised cages. The vanquished emerged in some unlikely places and guises: a U-boat flying a white flag sailed up New Hampshire's Piscataqua river, where bewildered state police received its captain and crew. Irish prime minister Eamonn de Valera, flaunting to the end his loathing of his British neighbours, paid a formal call upon the German Embassy in Dublin, to express his condolences on the death of the Reich's head of state.

Many Germans believed themselves as much victims of Hitler as were the foreign nations he had conquered and enslaved. In Hamburg, old Mathilde Wolff-Monckeburg wrote broken-heartedly on 1 May: 'Our beautiful and proud Germany has been crushed... And all this because of one man who had a lunatic vision of being "chosen by God".'

Among Germans in the summer of 1945 and afterwards, self-pity was a much more prevalent sensation than contrition: one in three of their male children born between 1915 and 1924 was dead, two in five of those born between 1920 and 1925. In the vast refugee migrations that preceded and followed VE-Day, more than 14 million ethnic Germans left homes in the east, or were driven from them. Meanwhile more millions of people of a dozen nationalities, enslaved by Hitler, entered a new dark tunnel of uncertainty in Displaced Persons camps administered by the Allies, where some remained for years. The least fortunate were summarily consigned to Russia, their nominal homeland, where many were categorised by the NKVD as proven or putative traitors, and killed.

In Germany's cities, half the housing stock had been destroyed. 'Nuremburg is a city of the dead,' wrote Richard Johnston of the *New York Times*. Berlin, Dresden, Hamburg were worse. The physical devastation of 1945 was unparalleled in history: Europe's great cities had been spared by the First World War and even by the rampages of Napoleon.

For two years after VE-Day, the NKVD waged a bloody counter-insurgency campaign in Poland and Ukraine, to impose Stalin's will upon peoples consumed with bitterness about exchanging Nazi tyranny for that of the Soviets. Exiled Poles in the West were dismayed to be denied a place in London's victory parade, because the new British Labour government declined to upset the Russians. General Wladsylaw Anders wrote: 'I felt as if I were peeping at a ballroom from behind the curtain of an entrance door through which I might not pass.'

His bitterness was justified. The Poles, who had fought gallantly with the Allied forces, ended the war as they began it, human sacrifices to the realities of power. The Americans and British had delivered half Europe from one totalitarian tyranny, but lacked the political will and military means to save 90 million people in the East from falling victim to a new, Soviet bondage that lasted almost half a century. The price of having joined with Stalin to destroy Hitler was high indeed.

In the victorious nations, simple people greeted the outcome of the struggle as a triumph of virtue over evil, heedless of the fashion in which liberation was blighted in many parts of the world. Painted high on the walls of several adjoining houses in housewife Edie Rutherford's Sheffield street were the words: GOD BLESS OUR LADS FOR THIS VICTORY. She and her friends spoke of Churchill: 'Everyone agreed that we have been well blest in having such a leader. I felt once again great gratitude for being born British.'

Millions of humble folk thought not of global issues, but of movingly personal causes for gratitude. On 7 September 1941, 19-year-old gunner Bob Grafton, an east Londoner, wrote to his adored girlfriend Dot before embarkation for the Far East:

Darling I *know* that you will wait for me. Darling do you know this. I swear that as long as we are apart I will never never touch another woman either physically or mentally. I do mean that Dot an awful lot... Yours Ever, with Love and Devotion so deep that the fires burn even in sleep, Bob.

Before Singapore fell, Grafton escaped by junk to Sumatra, then lived wild in the jungle until he was captured by the Japanese in March 1942. Having survived a bondage which included two years on the Burma railway, in September 1945 he wrote to Dot from a homeward-bound troopship:

This I know: that it was you of the two of us who had the more difficult task. For I am a man (perhaps prematurely) and men must fight and women must weep... Even if we have lost four years we'll make life so that it is never regretted.

Grafton's story had a happy ending: he married his Dot, and they lived happily ever after. Many others, however, returned home to discover that old ties were shattered, former passions extinct; they were obliged to content themselves with their own survival.

France, Britain and its dominions were the only major nations to enter World War II as an act of principle, rather than because they sought territorial gains or were themselves attacked. But most French people persuaded themselves in 1940 that the Petain regime constituted a lawful government; however uncomfortably, they indulged its rule until the eve of liberation in 1944. After the liberation, the French indulged an orgy of recrimination, together with a settling of national and local accounts between former collaborationists and resisters, which prompted several thousand killings during *l'epuration* – the purification, as it was ironically known. To this day, France has not produced an official history of its war experience and probably will never do so, because consensual support for any version of events would be unattainable.

It is hard to imagine that Britain would have continued to defy Hitler after June 1940 in the absence of Winston Churchill, who constructed a brilliant and narrowly plausible narrative for the British people, first about what they might do, and later to persuade them of what they had done. Churchill displayed the highest wisdom by embracing the Soviet Union as a co-belligerent in 1941, but both he – briefly – and later Roosevelt – persistently – were foolish to suppose that a real partnership was possible. Stalin, with his usual icy clarity of vision, recognised that the common commitment of Britain, Russia and the

US to defeat Hitler did nothing to bridge the yawning divide between their respective national objectives. Russia's vast blood sacrifice spared the lives of hundreds of thousands of British and American soldiers, but in consequence the Red Army secured physical possession of an East European empire.

There is a powerful argument that only a warlord as bereft of scruple or compassion as Stalin could have destroyed Nazism. He proved a supremely effective tyrant, as Hitler was not. The Western Allies' manner of fighting, hampered by bourgeois sensitivity about casualties, was a chronic impediment to overcoming the Wehrmacht.

Because German and Japanese soldiers displayed high courage and tactical skill, the principal Axis powers were overrated by their enemies. From June 1940 onwards, both Berlin and Tokyo made strategy with awesome incompetence. Whether or not the leaders of Germany and Japan were stupid men, they did many stupid things, often because their understanding of their opponents was so poor. Most of the men close to Hitler, Himmler and Goering notable among them, would have seemed to posterity ridiculous figures, save that they had licence to shed so much blood.

The war became a proud national folk memory, because the British came to regard it as the last hurrah of their greatness, an historic achievement to set against many postwar failures and disappointments. Their lone stand against Nazism in 1940-41 was indeed their finest hour, for which they were empowered by Winston Churchill, the towering personality of the forces of light. Throughout the war, Britain was governed with impressive efficiency. The Royal Navy and RAF did many things bravely and well, though always straining to match their strengths to their commitments. The British Army's overall performance never surpassed adequacy, and often fell short of it. As an institution, it was deficient in competent commanders, imagination, appropriate transport and armour, energy and professional skill, its artillery alone excluded.

The United States, whose industrial might contributed more to victory than did its armies, was the only belligerent which emerged from the war without a sense of victimhood. It was characteristic of American romanticism that a war which the United States joined only because it was attacked by Japan evolved during the ensuing 45 months into a 'crusade for freedom'.

The Russians emerged from the war conscious of their new power in the world, but also embittered by the colossal destruction and loss of life they had suffered. They believed, not mistakenly, that the Western Allies had purchased cheaply their share of victory, reinforcing their visceral sense of grievance towards Europe and the United States. They forgot their role as Hitler's Allies between 1939 and 1941. Modern Russia maintains a stubborn, defiant denial about the Red Army's 1944-45 orgy of rape, pillage and murder: it is deemed insulting that foreigners make much of the issue, for it compromises both the nation's cherished claims to victimhood, and the glory of its military triumph.

The impact of a conflict cannot be measured merely by comparing respective national tallies of human loss, but these deserve consideration, to achieve a sense of global perspective. There is no commonly agreed total of war-related deaths around the world, but a minimum figure of sixty million is accepted, and perhaps as many ten millions more. Russia lost twenty seven million people, China at least fifteen million. Germany lost 6.9 million dead, 5.33 million of these military. More than five million Poles died, most in German concentration camps, though the Russians could also claim a substantial tally of Polish victims. France lost 567,000 people, Britain 449,000. Total United States war losses were 418,500, slightly fewer than those of the UK.

Combatants fared better than civilians: around three-quarters of all those who perished were unarmed victims rather than active participants in the struggle. The peoples of Western Europe escaped more lightly than those of Eastern Europe. The best recent research suggests that 5.7 million Jews of all nationalities – out of a prewar Jewish population of 7.3 million in lands occupied by Hitler – were killed by the Nazis in their attempt to achieve a 'Final Solution'. Hitler's agents also murdered or allowed to die some three million Soviet PoWs; 1.8 million non-Jewish Poles; five million non-Jewish Soviet citizens; 150,000 mentally handicapped people; and some 10,000 gay men. Only a tiny fraction of those guilty of war crimes were ever indicted, partly because the victors had no stomach for the scale of executions, numbering several hundreds of thousands, which would have been necessary had strict justice been enforced against every Axis murderer.

Palestine was among the lands most conspicuously influenced by the outcome of the conflict. Never again would anti-Semitism be socially acceptable in western democratic societies; the slaughter of Europe's Jews precipitated the 1948 creation of the state of Israel. Yet widespread bitterness persists that the Western Powers assuaged their own guilt about the wartime fate of the Jews by making a great historic gesture in lands identified by Muslims as rightfully Arab.

Within Western culture, of course, the conflict continues to exercise an extraordinary fascination for generations unborn when it took place. The obvious explanation is that this was the greatest and most terrible event in human history. Within the vast compass of the struggle, some individuals scaled summits of courage and nobility, while others plumbed depths of evil, in a fashion that compels the awe of posterity. Among citizens of modern democracies to whom serious hardship and collective peril are unknown, the tribulations which hundreds of millions endured between 1939 and 1945 are almost beyond comprehension. It is impossible to dignify the struggle as an unalloyed contest between good and evil. Allied victory did not bring universal peace, prosperity, justice or freedom. All that seems certain is that Allied victory saved the world from a much worse fate that would have followed the triumph of Germany and Japan. With this knowledge, seekers after virtue and truth must be content.

BIBLIOGRAPHY

A comprehensive bibliography is unrealistic within the compass of these pages. I have listed here only titles on which I have drawn extensively for my own narrative, or which seem especially noteworthy for further reading. I have omitted to detail the multiple volumes of the British and American official histories, which are of course indispensable.

Atkinson, Rick *The Day of Battle* Henry Holt 2007
Barnett, Corelli *Engage The Enemy More Closely* Hodder & Stoughton 1991
Bayly, Christopher & Harper, Tim *Forgotten Armies* Penguin 2004
Beevor, Antony Stalingrad Viking 1998 *The Fall of Berlin 1945* Penguin 2002
Bellamy, Chris *Absolute War* Macmillan 2007
Belov, N. F. *Front Diary of N.F.Belov 1941-44*
Blair, Clay *Hitler's U-Boat Wars* Random House 1996
Blum, John Morton *V Was For Victory* Harcourt Brace 1976
Browning, Christopher *Ordinary Men* Penguin 1998
Calvocoressi, Peter, Wint Guy & Pritchard, John *Total War* Viking 1972
Dear I.C.B. & Foot M.R.D. eds. *The Oxford Companion To the Second World War* Oxford 1995
D'Este, Carlo *Decision In Normandy* Collins 1983
Djilas, Milovan *Wartime* Secker & Warburg 1980
Echternkamp, Jorg ed. *Germany And The Second World War* Research Institute For Military History Potsdam/Oxford 9 vols.1990-2008
Grossman, Vassili ed. Vinogradova, Lyuba & Beevor, Antony *A Writer At War* Harvill 2006
Halder, Franz *Command In Conflict: The Diaries And Notes of Colonel-General Franz Halder and other members of the German High Command* ed. Barry

Leach and Ian MacDonald Oxford 1985

Howarth, Stephen & Law, David ed. *The Battle of the Atlantic 1939-45* Greenhill 1994

Jackson, Julian *The Fall Of France* Oxford 2003

Jones, Michael, *The Retreat: Hitler's First Defeat* John Murray 2009; *The Siege of Leningrad* John Murray 2008

Killingray, David *Fighting For Britain* James Currey 2010

Klemperer, Victor *I shall Bear Witness* Weidenfeld & Nicolson 1999

Koa Wing, Sandra ed. *Our Longest Days* Profile 2008

Last, Nella *Nella Last's War* Sphere 1981

Longerich, Peter *Holocaust* Oxford 2010

MacGregor, Knox *Mussolini Unleashed, 1939-1941: Politics and Strategy in Fascist Italy's Last War* Cambridge University Press 1982

Mazower, Mark *Hitler's Empire* Penguin 2008

Merridale, Catherine *Ivan's War* Faber 2005

Moltke, Helmuth Von *Letters to Freya ed Beatte von Oppen* Collins Harvill 1991

Murray, Williamson *Luftwaffe* Allen & Unwin 1985

Overy, Richard *Why The Allies Won* Allen Lane 1995; *Russia's War* Allen Lane 1997

Payne, Stanley *Franco And Hitler* Yale 2008

Perrett, Geoffrey *Days of Sadness Years of Triumph* University of Wisconsin 1973; *Pisma S Ognennogo Rubezha 1941-1945 [Letters from the Front 1941-1945]* St. Petersburg, 1992; *Pisma S Viony* Ioshkar-Ola 1995

Smith, Colin *England's Last War With France: Fighting Vichy 1940-42* Wiedenfeld & Nicolson 2009; *Singapore Burning* Penguin 2005

Spector, Ronald *Eagle Against The Sun* Viking 1985

Sweetman, John *The Dambusters Raid* Arms And Armour 1993

Thorne, Christopher *The Issue of War* Oxford 1985; *Allies Of A Kind* Hamish Hamilton 1978

Tooze, Adam *The Wages Of Destruction* Penguin 2007

Vallicella, Vittorio *Diario di Guerra da El Alamein alla tragica ritirata 1942-1943* Edizioni Arterigere 2009

Weinburg, Gerhard *A World At Arms* Cambridge 1994

Wilmot, Chester *The Struggle For Europe* Wordworth 1997

Wolff-Monckeburg, *Mathilde On The Other Side* ed.Ruth Evans Pan 1979

Woodman, Richard *The Real Cruel Sea* John Murray 2004; *Arctic Convoys* John Murray 2001; *Malta Convoys* John Murray 2000

INDEX